Rescue Horses and Their Stories

The courageous journey of 14 magnificent horses

By

April Carlson-Depuy

Dedication

This book is dedicated to my husband, Don Depuy, rescuer and trainer of many abused and neglected horses. It is also dedicated to Charlotte Barks, Laurie Finch, Dawn Keene, and Nadine Hoy, all exceptional women who have unselfishly given their time to save hundreds of animals. It is also dedicated to all those others who are kind to animals and last but not least, to those mistreated animals who have been beaten down, but have had the courage to get back up and survive.

Table of Contents

Introduction

Don and April, 1998

Chapter 1: How It All Began

Just before Don and I married in 1998, I had purchased AAPiekna, a 17-year-old Polish Arabian broodmare. It's a good thing Don, a professional horseman, came into my life then because AAPiekna was still quite lively for an old girl. I wasn't experienced with horses and didn't know how to handle AAPiekna well. During our first few months of marriage, Don helped me learn to work with AAPiekna. Don and I then talked about acquiring a second horse so we could trail ride together.

Before we could pursue that plan, we received a life-changing call. A representative from the Humane Society contacted Don and asked if he would please help rescue 18 starved and neglected horses. The horses were so frightened that Humane Society volunteers couldn't catch them. They knew that Don was a good hand with horses and could catch them if anyone could.

Don hooked up his 4-horse stock trailer in case the Humane Society needed assistance delivering horses to their foster homes. We stopped and picked up neighbor, Vera Grey on our way to the rescue site. Vera was also a good hand with horses. The Humane Society needed all the help they could get. Don has always had a God-given gift to work with animals, especially horses. He also learned a lot about horse training from his grandfather, Don

Colwell. Don started helping his grandfather with horses at age 8 and continued throughout adulthood.

When we reached the Humane Society, horses were running around frantically in all directions, trying to avoid capture. It was obvious that they were terrified and didn't trust people. Don's demeanor was calm and confident. He was able to catch and halter all 18 horses. One little chestnut filly kept escaping her new foster parent. She ran right back to Don a total of 3 times and attached herself to his heels. As Don continued to catch other horses, this little filly continued to follow Don just like a dog. Each time Don handed her off to someone, she would break free and reattach herself to him (this was Puddin). Don finally gave up, picked up her lead rope, and hauled her along with him. All except a few horses were loaded in trailers and off to their new homes, so we prepared to leave. Don had his little filly. I was still holding a very skittish bay filly (Brook) and Vera was still holding a gray filly (LaSheena). Don said, "Well, I guess these three can go home with us for now."

As we led these three horses to the trailer, Don noticed an old white mare who had been left behind. I asked, "What are we going to do about her?" When Don saw her big sad eyes, he said, "I know better, but we can't leave her here all alone." "We might as well load her up, too." That old white mare was Whitey.

When we got home, Vera took the gray mare to her place. We unloaded our three and AAPiekna had three instant roommates. Our foster horses had received no food or water for over a month during a cold and brutal January, and their bodies were cannibalizing. Whether or not they would make it was yet to be determined, but we had to try. Don worked cautiously to rebuild the horse's health. They were hungry, but he knew overfeeding them would do more harm than good. We spent a lot of time trying to regain their trust. We groomed them, talked with them and showed the horses that we could be trusted. Slowly but surely, they began to put on healthy weight. They also began looking to us for attention. During their rehabilitation process, we were on pins and needles. We were concerned about the outcome of the horse's court custody case.

The court case was a long-drawn-out battle. The Palmers (owners) were acquitted due to the way the case was originally filed. Fortunately, the judge ruled in favor of the horses by decreeing that the Palmers had to pay a large sum of board money in order to get their horses back. They were not able to pay the fine and lost custody of their 18 horses and a bull. We all celebrated this outcome for the sake of the animals.

Top Photo: Don with Puddin on rescue day.

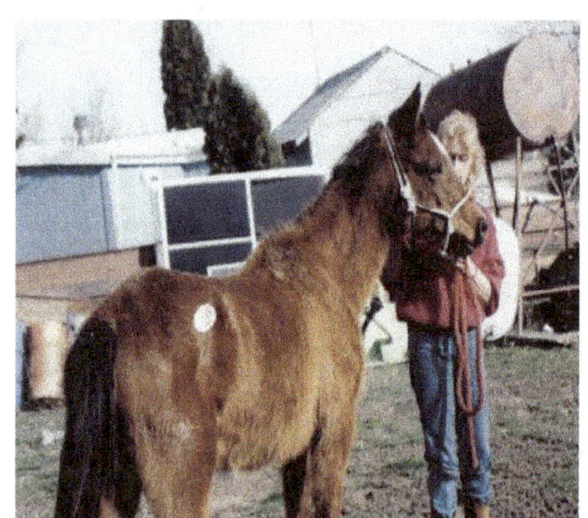

April with Brook and Vera with LaSheena on rescue day.

Palmers fail to pay; lose 19 animals

Humane society now owns horses and bull

By DOUG HIGGS
H&N Staff Writer

James and Mary Palmer have lost their 18 horses and a bull, even though they were exonerated of charges that they neglected the animals.

The Henley-area couple lost the animals Wednesday when they failed to pay $22,104 to the Klamath Humane Society for six months boarding costs incurred since the animals were seized by law enforcement authorities last March.

The animals now belong to the humane society, which reportedly intends to put them up for adoption.

Klamath County Circuit Judge Richard Rambo Wednesday denied a request by the Palmers to reconsider whether $22,104 was a fair charge for boarding costs.

The Palmers contended the costs were exaggerated, but Rambo said the matter had been settled after two previous hearings

The horses and bull have been in the custody of the humane society since they were seized March 13 at the Palmers' ranch of about 10-1/2 acres at 9332 Reeder Road.

The Palmers recently prevailed in a criminal case in which a jury acquitted them of 19 counts of second-degree animal neglect.

Despite the outcome of the criminal case, Oregon law requires the owners of the seized animals to pay the humane society for its expenses in caring for the animals while they were in the humane society's custody.

It was established in the trial that the horses and bull, which were in badly deteriorated physical condition when seized, have been restored to normal health since being taken to the humane society.

In acquitting the Palmers of the neglect counts, the jury apparently considered personal difficulties experienced by the Palmers during the time the physical condition of their animals deteriorated.

These included major surgery in which Palmer had a liver transplant early last February in Portland.

The Palmers, in the trial, said they did not want to see anything bad happen to their animals and wanted to have them back.

Humane society officials have vigorously opposed the return of the animals to the Palmers, predicting they would again neglect the animals if they were returned to them.

However, the Palmers can still regain possession of 12 sheep, which also were seized, if they pay the humane society $4,222. The Palmers were not accused of neglecting the sheep.

Thank You From The Animals

With appreciation, a bull, a flock of sheep, 18 horses, and the Klamath Humane Society wish to extend a thank you to numerous Klamath County individuals.

Without their support, the resources needed to restore each animal's health would have been limited!

The generosity of the foster parents, local veterinarians, Humane Society volunteers, and financial contributors, helped reconstruct and maintain the health of these malnourished animals.

If the animals could speak perhaps they would share the following message:

"The gentle cherishing of all forms of life comes with accepting life as a single community, sharing the same home and hearth."

On behalf of the animals, we offer a sincere thank you to everyone who cared and helped them!

A. S. Depuy
10/24/98

As the horses recovered, we discovered that they were pure-bred Arabian mares. They all had a tremendous amount of energy. These horses made it clear that they needed something constructive to do. I told Don that I heard Arabian horses excelled at a sport called "endurance" (long-distance cross country running). Once the horses were well, we decided to give endurance a try, and we all got hooked on the sport. The horses loved endurance running and so did we.

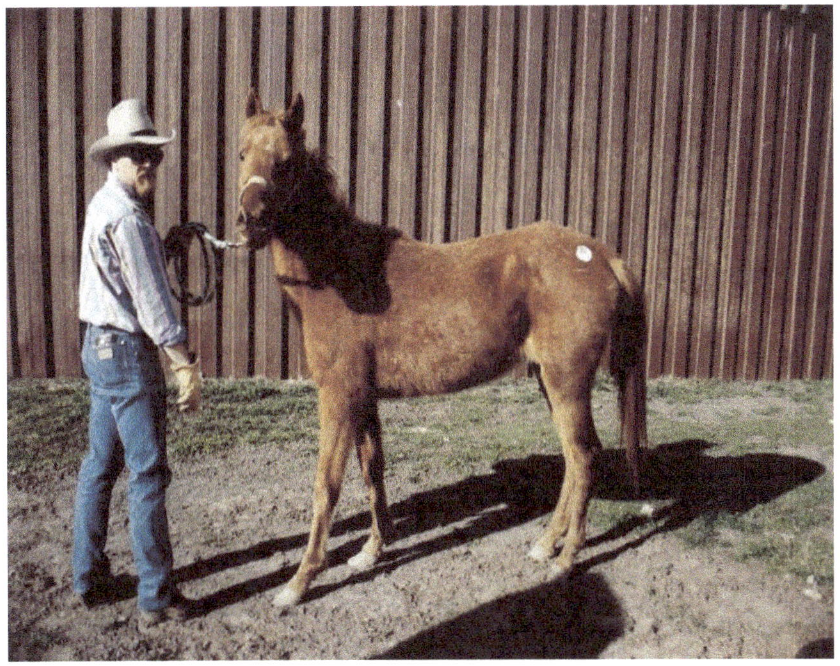

Puddin before recovery

Puddin at the Dunes Endurance ride after recovery

Photo by Joyce Brown

Puddin became an exceptional endurance horse. Today at age 27, she is still full of energy and running strong. Puddin has done a lot of amazing things in her lifetime such as rescuing a baby elk calf from a mud bog. One day, Don was riding Puddin out in the timber country northwest of our home. Puddin usually behaved quite well, but on this day, she was determined to go in a different direction than Don wanted her to. Puddin was so insistent that Don finally let her set the course. She led him straight to a terrified elk calf who was mired down in a mud bog. Don roped the calf, but the weight of Don and Puddin together was too much. Puddin and Don began to sink in the mud.

Don and Puddin hard at work

Don and Puddin herd cattle and a feral horse

Don hopped off, dallied the rope around the saddle horn and told Puddin to pull the calf out by herself. Puddin knew what to do. She backed up and pulled the bellowing baby to safety. The elk calf shook himself off and bellowed a few more times as he staggered through the woods in search of mama. Puddin saved the elk calf's life.

Puddin is an amazing little horse who has continued to do a lot to help us and other animals. Puddin thinks she is a great big horse although she is barely 700 pounds and 14 hands high. Puddin helped rehabilitate Don after he broke his leg. She also helped rehabilitate me after I broke my ribs. In addition, that tough little horse has hauled (ponied out) and helped us train many young horses three times her size. Puddin quickly learned how to work range cattle. One day, Puddin helped Don rope and dump a huge unruly 1,200-pound range steer like nobody's business. Puddin was willing to help Don chase and rope anything.

We had a young bear loitering around our neighborhood and Don became afraid for it. It was apt to get into someone's garbage and Don didn't want it to get shot. Don spotted the bear meandering along the trail next to our property so he saddled Puddin and they took off after it. The bear saw them coming and took off lumbering down the trail at high speed. Puddin joyfully charged after the bear, caught up to it, and Don roped it. They then drugged the shocked creature a few feet down the trail and turned it loose. The bear took off for the high country, bawling all the way. Don and Puddin hadn't hurt the guy. Don just wanted to scare him badly enough so he wouldn't come back towards the

neighborhood. It was doubtful that little fella was going to come visiting us ever again.

Don and Puddin at the Rogue River Endurance Ride

Photo by Joyce Brown

Puddin's greatest joy is to run fast. According to Puddin there is no bad footing. She can soar through rugged country like Pegasus at break-neck speeds. Using a GPS, we clocked Puddin running 45 mph which wasn't even her top speed. Puddin has served as Don's elk hunting partner and she loves the chase. Don and Puddin once spotted a bull elk during hunting season. Puddin took off after the elk before Don could get square in the saddle. They closed in and Don leaped off, aimed his rifle and YIKES! The elk was right there in range, but Don couldn't take the shot because Puddin was leaning over his shoulder, breathing heavy with excitement and fogging up his rifle scope! LOL! Puddin can be wild and crazy, but she has also taken good care of many children and given them riding lessons. Puddin is a great horse.

Chapter 2: Comeback from Injury, Thanks to Puddin

Puddin, our 24-year-old retired endurance horse, rehabilitated me, and I am humbly grateful. I wasn't sure I would ever ride a horse again after my horrendous horse wreck in October of 2019. As the story goes, Don and I were out riding Eufalla and Samie on trails near our home. Both mares are well trained, well-mannered and have a lot of limited distance and some endurance miles (25-to-50-mile cross country endurance races). We were just 500 yards from home when both horses suddenly blew up!

Samie started bucking wildly. Eufalla spun violently, not just once but several times. Both horses were terrified! I held my seat for the first violent spin or two and then I went flying off. I hit the ground hard! I had an equestrian protective vest on, but my vest laces up the sides and I skillfully landed on a large stick that poked me right between the laces. This resulted in broken ribs. My loyal little mare stopped the minute I hit the ground. Her reins were dangling and I didn't want her to run off. I'm not sure how, but I got to my knees and grabbed the loop reins with my right hand. Don's horse was still terrified and bucking so he couldn't help me.

The pressure of me grabbing the reins intensified Eufalla's fear. She added insult to insult by dragging me down the trail. I finally let go and fortunately, Eufalla didn't go far. Don was finally able to get off Samie and catch Eufalla.

Walking the 500 yards back home was a challenge. Anyone who has had broken ribs can well imagine how tough that was, plus my shoulder was damaged. Both horses continued to show terror all the way home so we knew something big had just happened. Later, Don went back to the scene of the accident to investigate. He discovered that there had been a predator in the brush. Tracks, scent and other signs showed it had been a wolverine, well known for being quite vicious.

Wolverines are not common to Southern Oregon, but Don thought one had migrated up the Klamath River canyon probably due to wildfires in northern California.

My injuries were serious and I was laid up for almost three months. I was able to sit in a director's chair, use a garbage grabber stick to pick things up, and take short slow walks, but that was about it. I had to hold as still as possible in order for my ribs to mend properly. I won't go into a description of how bad the pain was.

I did my best to maintain a positive attitude because I feel that one heals quicker and better if one stays positive. Still, I will probably never forget the misery I experienced that for three months, plus I had no opportunity to "get back in the saddle to overcome my fear!" It is interesting what the mind can do when fear is allowed to take over. I truly had no desire to get back on a horse again for the rest of my life. Well, there was a major problem with that train of thought. For one thing, we have eight horses of our own (all family members) and Don needs help from me to care for them. In addition, we were both hired the previous summer to train rescue horses for the Klamath Falls Large Animal Shelter (Humane Society).

I have commitments and responsibilities to horses and people so letting fear overtake my mind was not a good option. After my ribs healed, I started taking a strength-building class at our local YMCA. By early spring, I regained much of my strength and stamina. Don and I discussed the best way for me to get back in the saddle. We thought entering a 10-mile trail ride at a spring endurance event would be a good way for me to overcome my fear, before trying a longer more competitive endurance ride. We also thought me riding Puddin, our 24year-old retired endurance horse, was another good idea. Well, Puddin rehabbed me all right! I was not expecting the wild but amazing adventure she took me on! That little Arabian mare gave me no choice but to regain my confidence. God Bless that little horse!

I have had over 40 years of horse-riding experience, plus I have assisted Don, a professional horse trainer, for over 20 years now. I like to think of myself as an experienced equestrian and rider, so it was not easy for me to admit that I was now terrified of horses. I was even afraid to work with them from the ground. Getting back on one felt even more terrifying. Well, once again, Puddin's antics definitely got me past my fear. As mentioned above, we were just signed up to do a ten-mile trail ride at an endurance event in May.

The first surprise is that the ten-mile turned out to be an obstacle course event and 20 miles instead of 10. The thought of dealing with obstacles on the trail intensified my fear even more. To top things off, Puddin thought she was back at an endurance race and her energy was higher than a kite. So much for me riding a calm older horse on a 10-mile pleasure ride. Describing Puddin as enthusiastic is putting it mildly. Honestly, we have seldom seen Puddin that high up with her energy.

When I first stepped up on Puddin, she was bouncing from one side of the ride camp to the other. I was absolutely petrified and I had to get off. She truly was very close to being OUT OF CONTROL! Puddin's out-of-control behavior was not due to misbehavior or lack of training. It was due to her extreme excitement about coming out of retirement and being back in what she thought was the competitive game of endurance. I told Don I was too frightened to ride her. I couldn't seem to shake my fear and she was an extreme handful. As I tried to ride Puddin, she actually leaped into the air like a Lipizzaner and she was not listening to me at all. Don was supportive and did not pressure me to ride her. I knew in my heart that if I did not ride Puddin on this trail ride that I would NEVER get on a horse EVER again.

Puddin was quite thrilled to be out of retirement!

More important, Puddin was so excited about coming out of retirement that it broke my heart to think I might let her down. At the same time, I had a big decision to make. "Was it foolish to try to ride a horse that was out of control?" Well, of course, we all know the answer to that. Yes, of course, it was so I got off faster than the speed of light. I hope I don't sound too religious, but I went into the living quarters' horse trailer and prayed about it.

I asked, "Was it time for me to quit riding horses, or did God want me to continue helping Don with them?" The answer came and I was terrified once again. I then said, "Okay, God so you do still want me to ride horses." "Well, could you then please help me face this intense fear?" This may sound far-fetched to some and perhaps not to others, but right after praying and meditating, a great sense of peace came over me. I felt very calm as I walked out and said, "Don, I need to do this for Puddin's sake, our other horse's sake and for my own!" Don said, "Okay then!" He proceeded to instruct me to do ground work with Puddin, to be firm and make her mind! I put my fear aside (it was still there, but I made myself ignore it) and I was firm with Puddin on the ground. Once I took command, Puddin settled right down or at least enough to allow me to get back on her.

Off we went and Puddin became the most intense jackhammer on the planet! Well, I was committed by then. Puddin bounced intensely for the next 10 miles or more. We sure hadn't expected the course to be 20 miles long. We had started out at 5:00 p.m. and had to trot and then run the last eight miles to get back before dark. We still did not get back until 9:30 p.m. and YIKES, it was dark by then! That was a new experience for me because I had never ridden in the dark before. I learned that horses see quite well in darkness. Having to trust my horse in the dark was another confidence builder!

Puddin was THRILLED! She took the lead when we began trotting and she ran like a powerhouse. She really stretched out in her long trot. Samie had to lope to keep up with Puddin's trot. I did my best to manage Puddin and not let her overdo it. She had an absolute ball, though and once again; I had no choice but to regain my self-confidence. I, too, had a good time and so did Don and Samie. The last part of our ride was high up on a plateau. The view of the mountains just before dusk was absolutely stunning. This might have been Puddin's last big hurrah, but I doubt it. Puddin's enthusiasm and happiness were contagious. It truly was a beautiful ride.

We also had some comic relief on this ride. They say laughter is good for the soul. I learned that laughter is also good for overcoming one's fear. The first obstacle challenge on this so-called 10-mile event involved riding your horse up to a fence, gently removing a large yellow raincoat from the fence and then replacing it carefully further on down the fence line without spooking the horse.

Puddin reluctantly did the task for me, but she made it clear that she wanted to get going and run fast. I imagined Puddin to say, "Quit playing with the coat would ya!" Puddin made me throw the raincoat.

So how did she do this? Well, just as I was trying to gently lay the coat on the fence, Puddin danced and spun around. This caused me to throw the coat in a frenzy. The coat landed clear over on the other side of the fence. That didn't win us any points for the obstacle course competition, but the ride photographers caught the comical moment. As the coat went flying through the air, Puddin took off like a bat out of hell. She went flying off with a big grin on her old horsey face! I had no choice but to ride like the wind in order to stay with her!

It was a true blessing to give Puddin a wonderful endurance experience again, plus she really did rehabilitate me. Puddin helped me overcome my fear of riding horses, especially energetic ones. Thanks to Puddin, I gained enough confidence to move forward and to ride Eufalla again. I was even able to get back to helping Don work with troubled horses. God Bless Puddin! She is a great little soul and who knows? Puddin may just come out of retirement again soon.

Photos by Kelsey & Bo Shane, "Out of Steam Photography"

COURAGE IS RESISTANCE TO FEAR, MASTERY OF FEAR, NOT ABSENCE OF FEAR

April and Puddin, Don & Samie at the Prineville Endurance Event

Photo by Kelsey Shane, "Out of Steam Photography" May 2020

Chapter 3: Whitey, A Young Girl's Dreams Come True

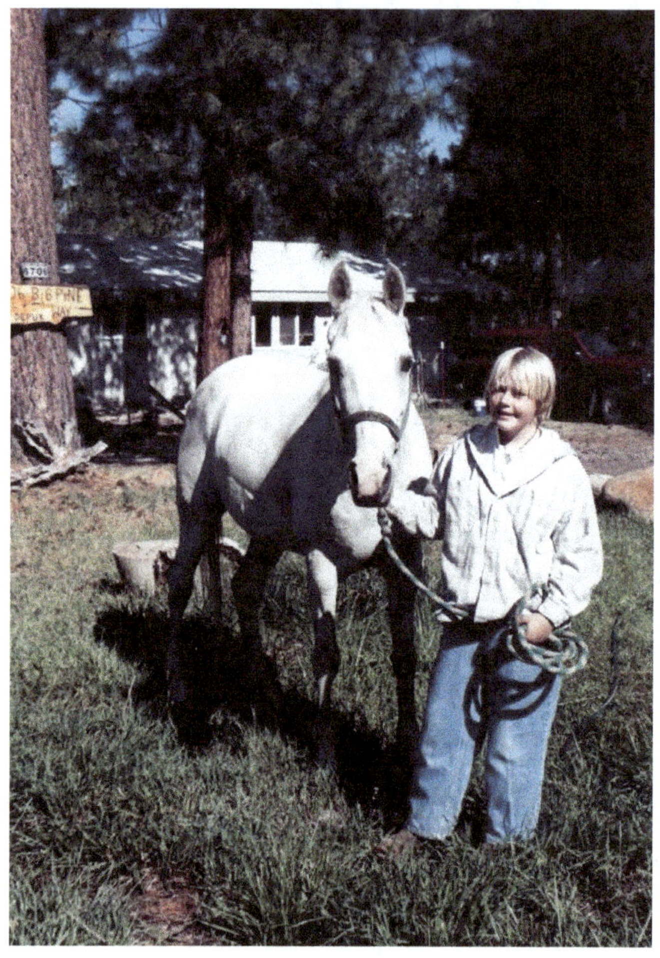

Whitey and her friend, Colleen Buck

Whitey was one of our original rescue horses. She was 18 years old when she first came to live with us, but she had the spirit of a young horse. Bing Tanga was her registered name and she originally came from an Arabian breeding farm in Orville, California. The owner had leased Whitey out to the Palmers and was unaware of her poor treatment. When she learned the story, she agreed to let us keep Whitey.

Whitey was a wonderful old mare. She took good care of several young girls who we mentored over the years. She was good-natured and even let Bo, our Border Collie pup grab her lead rope and take her on walks. Don and Whitey had a special bond. He often rode her up in the hills, where they both found peace and solace. We entered Whitey in a couple of endurance events. She was a beautiful runner, but long-distance running wasn't her thing. Whitey had a good home with us for 6 years until old age caught up with her. She is greatly missed.

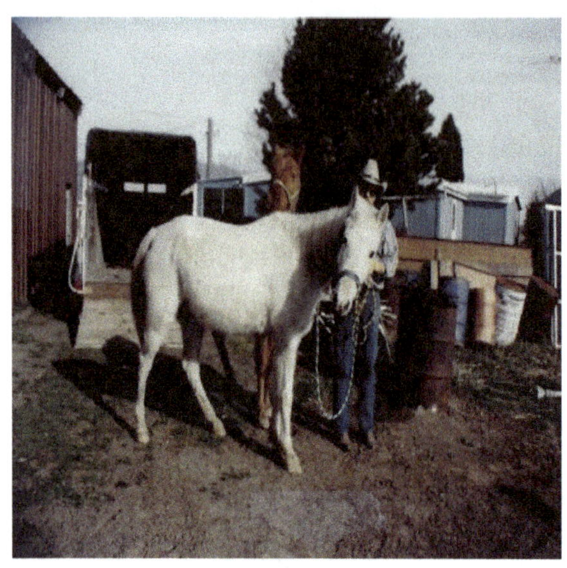

Top: Don with Whitey & Puddin on rescue day.
Bottom: April and Whitey at the Sunriver Endurance ride.
Photo by Joyce Brown.

DON AND WHITEY HAD A SPECIAL CONNECTION.

35

"A lovely horse is always an experience. It is an emotional experience
of the kind that is spoiled by words." - Beryl Markham

 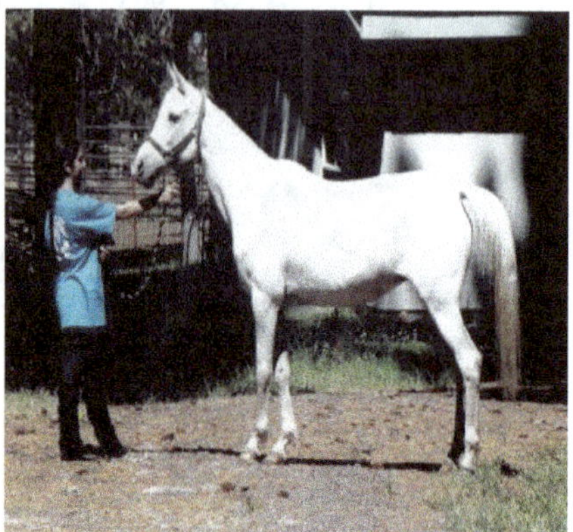

Whitey was very patient with children and other animals.

Bo Enjoyed taking Whitey for a walk.

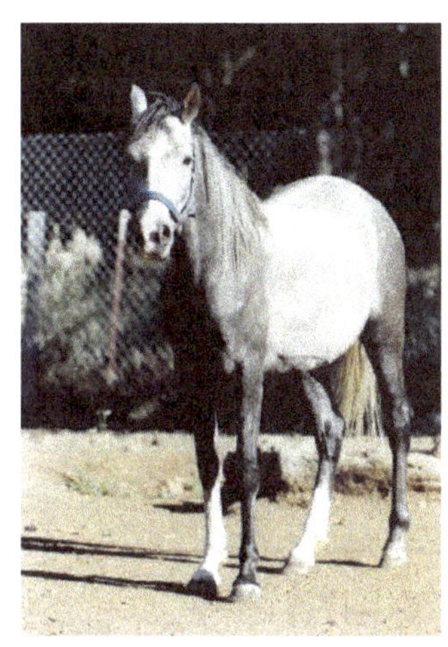

Top left: Vera & LaSheena on rescue day.
Right: LaSheena after recovery.
Bottom left: April & Brook on rescue day.
Right: Brook after recovery.

Neighbor Vera Grey rehabilitated LaSheena and took exceptionally good care of her. Due to financial reasons, Vera had to re-home LaSheena three years later. According to Vera, LaSheena ended up in a very good home. Brook was beautiful and athletic. We were able to rehabilitate Brook physically, but her mind was never right. Sadly, and with regret, we had to have Brook put down. Even though Don assures me we did the right thing, putting Brook to rest still haunts me.

Chapter 4: AAPiekna, A Whole Lot More

AAPiekna was a retired 17-year-old brood mare who I purchased from Tezea Mills-Collins in 1997. Tezea wanted her to have a safe home. Due to AAPiekna's famous Polish Arabian bloodlines, Tezea was concerned that others might try to have AAPiekna bred again. According to Tezea, AAPiekna experienced serious complications birthing her last foal. She had me promise not to have AAPiekna bred and I agreed.

It is doubtful that AAPiekna had much of a life before coming to live with us. Her life mainly consisted of being bred and having one foal after another. Her main exercise involved being attached to a hot walker and plodding along in circles. Her true nature was spunky and she had much untapped potential. AAPiekna showed a desire to become something more. AAPiekna seemed to enjoy our trail rides and she took good care of me.

Before meeting Don, I was not well experienced with horses. One fine day, AAPiekna and I went out on a trail ride and I promptly became lost and disoriented. We were 5 miles out in the woods west of home. I let AAPiekna have her head. She had a great built in GPS compass and safely got me back.

Another time out, some drunken punks stopped their pickup and started shooting at a tree right next to us. They laughed as they continued to shoot, probably hoping AAPiekna would buck me off. AAPiekna was unhappy about this, but she remained cool and kept me on her back. Fortunately, I was carrying a pistol and told the drunks to piss off or I would start shooting back. They must have taken my threat seriously because they quickly left and AAPiekna got me home safe and sound once again.

I met Don a few months after acquiring AAPiekna. He agreed that she had untapped potential so he helped me train and condition her. AAPiekna showed an unbelievable strength. We decided to give her a try as an endurance horse. She took to it and excelled in Limited Distance endurance events (25-to-30-mile cross country horse races). AAPiekna proved to be a steady and strong runner. She would get into a nice even trot and run smoothly all day long without tiring.

AAPiekna showed that retirees don't have to quit on life. AAPiekna was a great endurance horse and competed until she was 27 years old. We were very proud of her. She delighted in letting me know who was really the boss though. AAPiekna loved endurance events and also our trail rides up in the mountains. She especially loved her rewards of grain and carrots after working out. In fact, she loved them so much that she acquired the nick name of "Miss Piggy!"

AAPiekna and April at the Dunes Endurance ride.
Photo by Joyce Brown

As mentioned before, I was pretty naive about horses when AAPiekna and I began our first experiences together. She never let me forget that she knew more than me. In fact, AAPiekna was proficient at making our decisions.

One time, we were at the Rogue River Endurance ride when AAPiekna taught me quite a lesson. We came to the Rogue River and AAPiekna said, "I don't want to get wet." I insisted that we cross the river. She insisted that we NOT! I urged her forward. She backed up. I became more insistent and got her to take 2 steps into the icy swift current. We both locked horns. I gave AAPiekna a swift kick and she said, "Okay then!" "You go swimming." "Not me!"

AAPiekna proceeded to balk, spin and dump me in the river. She then ran back to the bank, stopped and watched the show. Don said all one could see were my two boots sticking straight up out of the water. I went completely under! When I came up, I heard AAPiekna say, "See what happens when you try to cross the river, dumbie!"

Well, Don and Puddin drug reluctant AAPiekna across the river where they waited for me to splash across. When I reached the far bank, I climbed on AAPiekna who then said, "April, you are wet and disgusting!" "Do I have to carry you on my back?" "Didn't I tell you not to cross that river." "I think you should walk!"

Fortunately, AAPiekna took pity on me and gave me a ride the last 10 miles back to camp. As we trotted down the trail, water squirted out of my boots and I was plastered with dust and mud. When we got to the finish line, I took off my sunglasses. I looked like a raccoon. AAPiekna looked great.

AAPiekna really taught me a lot. She was a magnificent horse. She proved that she was capable of being a lot more than a brood mare who just walked around in circles during her free time. We loved going on trail and endurance adventures together. She was also kind to many children. AAPiekna was gentle with kids and gave them safe rides. She was also very good with conning carrots from them. God called her home at age 30. I sure miss her.

AAPiekna tried to tell me that swimming in cold water was no fun!

AAPiekna was a powerful runner

AApiekna with her friends Jason & Jennifer

Photo by Joyce Brown

AAPiekna conning a carrot from friend, Brian

AAPiekna and past owner, Tezea Mills-Collins

Tezea, a young Irish woman, raised in South Africa came to the United States and became a race track jockey. She migrated to Oregon where she met and married Ron Collins. They started a horse farm near Chiloquin, Oregon. Tezea purchased AAPiekna from an Arabian breeding farm in Texas and only attempted to breed her once or twice before AAPiekna had difficulties. AAPiekna's career as a brood mare had mainly taken place in Texas before Tezea acquired her. Tezea and Ron eventually divorced. Tezea moved back to South Africa and from what I understand, has remarried. AAPiekna is a great aunt to Amistadd, my gelding, and his half-sister, Eufalla.

"Smile for the camera!"

AAPiekna and Tezea

Chapter 5: Amistadd and His Adventures

"A horse doesn't care how much you know until he knows how much you care. Put your hand on your horse and your heart in your hand."

-Pat Parelli-

Amistadd is an Arabian gelding we purchased as an endurance horse for me. He was an unbroke 5-year-old when we bought him from a breeding farm at a bargain price. We should have known better, but fortunately the rough start Amistadd and I had turned out well in the long run. When we drove up to the stables, 30 beautiful Polish Arabian mares ran up to the fence line to check us out. As we continued down the driveway, they all turned and dashed off except for one. A bay stood there staring at me. We drove slowly through the entrance and were surprised that the bay horse walked along the fence line keeping pace with us.

I commented, "Don, I think that horse is picking me out!" "He is trying to connect with me!" "Maybe we ought to look at that one instead of this Amistadd horse." "That horse is definitely connecting with you," Don remarked in agreement.

Robbin, the owner and breeder (a very nice person) greeted us and went to catch the horse who had been following me. You can imagine my surprise when she said, "This is Amistadd!" From the start, Amistadd made it clear that he was choosing "me." Our bond was instant. He was my horse and I was his person. He seemed nice and calm. Robbin motivated Amistadd to run around his corral. He showed that he was a beautiful and powerful mover. It's a good thing we were meant for one another because otherwise, I don't think I could have hung in there with him during the frustrating years ahead.

Amistadd was a different horse by the time we got home. The nice calm gelding we met at the Arabian farm transformed into a wild and crazed bronc when we unloaded him. He was not the same horse. We wondered if he had been given a sedative the day, we met him? A year later, Robbin and John, her associate revealed that Amistadd had originally been sold to some people who abused him for several years. Robbin and John care very much about their horses so they demanded Amistadd back when they discovered he was being mistreated.

I respect Robbin and John. They are both very caring people.

Perhaps they didn't realize just how badly Amistadd had been wounded from his mistreatment when they sold him to us. We just wish we had received this information upfront. We would have approached his training much differently. As it was, the day after we got home, I began Amistadd's training program too soon. WHAT A FIASCO!

Amistadd was one skittish guy! He eyed me nervously, but a few weeks later, I was able to saddle him. Amistadd reluctantly allowed this, but one day something spooked him. His lead rope was tied to a tire hooked to a tree for flex and give. Amistadd, quite a powerful boy pulled back so hard that the rope holding the tire broke. The tire hit the ground with a thud and Amistadd stepped right in the middle of it.

What are the odds that the tire would get stuck on a front leg (the right one to be exact)? Amistadd thought he was attacked! He panicked and tore off with the tire flopping and beating the heck out of him. I yelled, "WHOA, Amistadd!" He stopped for a second and seemed to plead with me to help him! I tried to approach him calmly. As I came near, he freaked and tore off into the yard. The faster he ran, the harder the tire slapped him. The more it beat, the more he panicked. I can't blame him for going nuts. Before I could catch Amistadd, he ran blindly into a wire fence. He fell down on his back and became totally trapped and encased in the wire. He was a tangled-up mess!

By now, I felt pretty crazed myself. Fortunately, I kept enough wits about me to sprint to the tack shed and grab wire cutters. Amistadd was laying there deathly still when I got back. Only 2 or 3 minutes had passed, but if felt like an eternity. I cut the goat wire that was entrapping him as fast as I could. By now, I too was horrified. Once free of the wire and tire, he leaped up like a volcanic eruption. He stopped and briefly glanced at me. It was as though he was thinking, "IT'S STILL AFTER ME!"

Amistadd then ran down the trail with a loose saddle about ready to turn and flank him. Once again, I tried to get him to stop, but before I could reach him the saddle twisted under his belly. He was FLANKED! Amistadd jumped and the saddle flopped and beat him worse than the tire had done. The saddle cinch did a great job of flanking him like a rodeo bucking bronc. By now Amistadd was MAD!!! Yes, I got to see what "really mad" looks like on a horse! I stood there helpless as he bucked hard and furiously all the way down the trail. The saddle finally went flying. Did he stop there? Heck no. He then proceeded to stomp and trash the heck out of my saddle, finally satisfied that he had killed "the cruel thing!" I thought for sure that he was going to run off into the woods, but somehow, he knew where he belonged. Amistadd ran back to his pasture and just stood there at the gate waiting for me to let him back in. He was still pretty mad at me and I am sure he was thinking, "How could you do this to me you dumb woman!"

The next ten years were tough. Fortunately, Don and I were as stubborn as Amistadd. We often felt like giving up, but it never felt right to quit him. Besides being stubborn, he also showed that he was an intelligent horse with a lot of heart. During our time working with Amistadd he showed us that he has a sense of humor and is quite a character. He is an enigma indeed.

Early Training Fun with Amistadd (LOL)

May 22, 2007

We continued to work hard with Amistadd. He began making progress, but he still became upset in tight quarters such as the round pen. We learned that part of Amistadd's mistreatment had involved people forcing him into tight quarters. They used bars and put intense pressure on both sides of him which created fear and compounded his trust issues.

Don had ridden Amistadd in the round pen by himself a few times, but even though he made some improvement, Amistadd still got quite jumpy. On this particular day, Don asked me to ride AAPiekna and lead Amistadd with a rope in the round pen. Don's intention was to ride Amistadd as we led them in a few circles.

When Don first mounted Amistadd, he made a mistake and goosed him sharply with the toe of his boot. RODEO! We should have sold tickets to the neighborhood. Amistadd started bucking like a crazy wild horse. I tried to reel them in by pulling the rope tight and dallying it to the saddle horn, but Amistadd was so powerful that he pulled me right out of the saddle. The centrifugal force sent me flying into the round pen bars head first. You should have seen the dent in the bars! Man, I love that cheap Walmart skate board helmet I was wearing. It was a dandy and it didn't have a dent nor did my head.

The entire incident happened so darn fast! Then after I was slam dunked into the round pen fence, I flew back the other way and landed underneath AAPiekna. AAPiekna carefully danced right over the top of me without touching me, God Bless her! At the same time, Amistadd started a bucking fit. Right then, Don's right rein broke which caused him to lose some control. With his new found freedom, Amistadd really turned up the crank.

Don could have ridden Amistadd out, but when I lost the rope and he jerked me out of the saddle, the rope burned fire across Don's chest. This instantly pulled Don right out of the saddle and thumped him to the ground. Don was stuck underneath Amistadd, the massive kicking machine who continued to buck furiously in one place; RIGHT OVER THE TOP OF DON! Don managed to punch him in the belly so he wouldn't get trampled and thank goodness, Amistadd moved forward. YIKES! He then leaped towards me, still bucking like a maniac.

Hitting the ground and round pen panels so hard had knocked the wind right out of me. For a minute or so I was physically paralyzed from the blow and couldn't move period. WHOA! What a weird feeling to have no motor skills for a few seconds (it felt like several minutes). Don, thank goodness has rapid thinking skills and the physical ability for a quick recovery. He jumped up instantly and grabbed Amistadd's lead rope just a few seconds before the brute reached me with his full bucking force!

By then, I was finally able to move (in slow motion it felt like) to the round pen panels. I frantically clung to the rails and hugged the heck out of them for support. Within a few minutes I could breathe again just as Don caught the big booger and settled him down. Don asked me how I landed out of the saddle in the first place. My first reaction was to say, AAPiekna bucked me off. AAPiekna was standing there facing me being good as gold. She was not being held by anyone or anything.

You should have seen the look she gave me the instant I said she "bucked me off." I could swear she said, "What do you mean? I am a good girl and it wasn't me!" The truth then dawned on me and I praised AAPiekna for being so good.

AAPiekna said, "I deserve a pay raise!"

I admitted to Don that the rope pulled me right off the saddle when Amistadd went to bucking and I wasn't smart enough to let go. I was actually trying to help Don and thought I could pull that big brute in, but I guess he did outweigh me by a few pounds. LOL! I can't begin to tell you how stiff and sore I was after that. That round pen dirt was hard packed. I had scrapes from one end to the other, a sore neck, shoulders, lower back, knee and calf. Well, Cowboy Don totally believes in the "Cowboy Up" philosophy. He also believes in "Cowgirl Up" as well.

Don wasn't going to force me, but he sure hoped I would get back in the saddle right away and do another go around with AAPiekna as my trusty mount. I agreed which surprised myself and him as well.

I slowly and painfully climbed back on AAPiekna. Please don't ask how I got on her as stiff and sore as I was. Both AAPiekna and I looked at naughty Amistadd and shook our heads. Don went to the tack shed to get some new reins since Amistadd's had broken during his fit. While Don was gone, I spoke calmly to Amistadd who was still quite stirred up. Using a quiet voice, I told Amistadd that we forgave him, but he had to do better this next time. The more soothing my voice became the more he settled down. It dawned on me that he was scared and had not bucked out of meanness. No doubt being goosed in the belly freaked him out.

When Don came back, I stuffed my fears into the deep recesses of my mind. Don showed me how to hold the rope at a different angle and how to block and support Amistadd using AAPiekna. When he climbed back into the saddle it felt like my heart stopped completely for several beats. Amistadd took several wicked jumps, but Don reined him in. This time, AAPiekna and I blocked Amistadd really well. WHEW! What a relief! Amistadd behaved and we proceeded to make three successful laps around the round pen with AAPiekna leading him at a snail's pace. AAPiekna only had two walking paces: 1. Slow snail and 2. Slower snail.

Don got on and off Amistadd several more times and then called it good for the day. Even though Amistadd had settled down after the 2nd lap, he never did lose the bow in his neck. Amistadd didn't get any grain after his lesson that morning which upset him pretty badly. I am pretty sure he knew why he didn't get his reward. Don said that we won this round and not Amistadd. He thanked me for being willing to get back in the saddle again. I wondered to myself if I was really brave or just plain nuts.

I had surgery on my knee the previous spring. For a while, I thought my knee was a goner again. I was frightened about that, but two days later, I was feeling back to normal other than my shoulders and neck were so stiff that I had to sleep with a special pillow. A few days later, I felt fine. Cowboy Don was stiff in the shoulders, but his bad leg held together so we were both grateful that we came out of that wreck in one piece. It is kind of funny now that I look back. We both got unloaded in the round pen, of all places. I thought, "better in there than out in the wilds, though."

Well, we went right back to working with Amistadd the next weekend. I was tempted to run and hide somewhere. Then again, I didn't want the devil to win so I dug up some courage and convinced myself not to give up on that horse. Don asked me to have faith so that's what I did. I also went to the ranch store and bought one of those special protective rodeo vests for our next go around in the round pen.

I told myself to never get lazy and take off my riding helmet and protective vest when riding any horse. It took 12 years of consistent hard work, faith and not giving up, but finally Amistadd turned the corner. We purchased Amistadd in 2002. Seventeen years later in 2019, Amistadd finally gave us his trust and became the most awesome horse I have ever encountered. When Amistadd gave us his trust, he also showed who he really is; a kind, loyal and beautiful animal.

Note: Amistadd's true nature becomes evident in the following story

Amistadd Becomes a Godfather

When Don got home from work on Monday, March 19, 2007, he noticed that Amistadd was rapidly pacing by his pasture gate in a frenzy. He was also making very odd contortions with his head and neck. Don described Amistadd's unusual behavior as throwing his head consistently in one direction which was north. Don glanced at Amistadd again as he approached the house. Don didn't pay much attention to Amistadd's pacing until he stepped up on the porch.

Amistadd's repetitive head tossing escalated. He was doing his best to say, "Don, we've got a problem over there" "Hey, Yo, Don, I'm talking." "Come back here please!"

Not comprehending yet, Don proceeded on into the house. As Don put his lunch pail away, he heard a loud commotion out back. He looked out the window and saw Amistadd going ballistic. He was now throwing his head and neck violently, but still in a northerly direction only. In addition, Amistadd began frantically racing back and forth from the gate to the north edge of the fence line. This struck Don as odd because when upset, Amistadd typically runs laps around his pasture. He doesn't run back and forth in a straight line.

Don suddenly realized that Amistadd was trying to tell him something. Amistadd's behavior became more frantic so Don raced out the back door. As Don entered his pasture, Amistadd ran ahead of him to the north fence line and stopped. Don was close behind him.

Amistadd stood by the fence and danced in place without going anywhere. Don caught up, looked over the fence and was stunned to see a doe down and struggling to give birth.

The doe was laying in the grass next to the fence and under some pine trees. The poor doe was desperately trying to let nature take its course. She was struggling and the fawn was not coming. Having once been a farmer/rancher in years past, Don had helped deliver many farm animals. He recognized the signs of an animal in trouble. The fawn was breech and couldn't make it out.

"This can't be much different from helping an ewe deliver a lamb," Don thought. Don hopped over the fence before he could talk himself out of it. The doe was temporarily paralyzed from the breech and had no choice but to let Don help her. He reached in, turned the fawn and pulled the baby out.

Amistadd watched the whole ordeal and did a Mexican hat dance when the fawn came out. Thanks to Amistadd and Don, baby Bambi successfully entered the world. Amistadd continued to watch and stand nearby. A few minutes after the birth, Amistadd bowed his majestic head and elegantly ran his laps around the pasture. Amistadd showed that he deeply cares. He couldn't settle down until things were right again with nature.

Moving Forward

During Amistadd's initial training period, I often got home too late from work to be of much help except on occasional weekends. During the first 3 years of his training, Don enlisted Janica Nowak, a high school girl to help him work with Amistadd. Don would saddle Amistadd and then Janica would climb on and off Amistadd in the round pen. Don controlled Amistadd from the ground and Janica served as the monkey. They advanced to short wild rides with Don holding the lead rope and barely maintaining the control.

Don and Puddin leading brave Janica on Amistadd

When Janica went off to college, I did my best to get home from work earlier. I rode Amistadd in the round pen with Don still controlling him from the ground. I felt like I was riding TNT explosives! My job and temporary health issues began to interfere. I could no longer consistently work with Amistadd. Don announced that he had done everything he could to help Amistadd during the past 12 years. He said, "I'm done!" "There is nothing more I can do for him." I didn't want Amistadd to become just a pasture ornament. I wasn't sure what to do so I prayed about it. The following November of 2011, I was led to Vanessa Hansen, a Christian cowgirl and horse trainer. Vanessa was exceptionally busy, so she recommended Marie Trzeczak, a talented 20-year-old horse trainer from Germany.

We invited Marie out to meet Amistadd. Amistadd liked Marie which was a miracle since he shied away from almost everyone else. Marie had once lived in Saudi Arabia where she learned to understand and work with Arabian horses. Marie was a Godsend and a blessing. Marie boarded Amistadd at the fairgrounds and she worked with him in a large indoor arena for a month. Amistadd continued to respond well to her. Marie did some finish work and great training with Amistadd. She also helped him learn to deal with the chaos and commotion at the fairgrounds.

Amistadd probably associated the fairgrounds with a hornet's nest. Although Amistadd liked Marie, he did not like living at the fairgrounds and nearly tore his stall down. He seemed very happy to get home at the end of his months training ordeal.

Marie did a wonderful job with Amistadd

Marie, an amazing young woman!

Marie and Michael

A few years later, Marie Trzeczak married Michael Merkley and became Mrs. Merkley. Marie is an amazing equestrian and a unique individual. She impressed her wedding guests by driving her bridesmaids to her own wedding in a horse drawn carriage! Marie is a very caring person who has a special way with horses. Amistadd and I were fortunate to have had her help.

After Amistadd came home, I took over working with him, but he was still resistant and ran away whenever I approached. Fortunately, I was retired from my career by the time Amistadd came back home that December of 2011. I began doing ground work and trust building with Amistadd 5 days per week regardless of the weather. At first, he resisted. I had to entice him with a bucket of grain in order to catch him. We worked in his pasture and did a lot of ground work. We wove around trees and practiced, "stop, go right, turn, left turn, whoa and back up." I also brushed and rubbed him all over whether he liked it or not.

68

Marie drove her bridesmaids to her wedding.

Amistadd continued to act like a wild man and would spook and jump at everything including his shadow. I worked with him at 1:00 p.m., at the same exact time each day. After 2 months of consistent ground work, it felt like we weren't getting anywhere. One day, I felt discouraged so I went in the house and looked out the window instead of working with him. Much to my surprise, Amistadd started rattling his gate at exactly 1:05 p.m. When I didn't show up, he continued to rattle his gate all the harder. I had a revelation. I grabbed his halter, lead rope and a bucket of grain, and went out to see him. I said, "Hey, big man!" "You're nothing but a big bluff" You do like working with me!"

He let me catch him and from that point on, I didn't allow any of his antics to bother me. We then both relaxed after that and moved forward together. Amistadd and I continued making progress. He even quit acting like a crazy man when we did our ground work routines. He began to look to me for reassurance whenever he was legitimately frightened of something. With God's help and Don's support, I started riding Amistadd in April of 2012. The first time I got on him, I said a prayer and tossed my fear aside. I put on my helmet and equestrian protective vest, took a homeopathic stress mint, saddled Amistadd and climbed up on his back before I could talk myself out of it.

The moment, I put my foot in the stirrups, Amistadd sprung up on his tip toes and I felt like I was going to be launched. I refused to allow myself to become scared. I knew we had to get through this. I took a deep breath, stuffed my fear again, relaxed my body and Amistadd then settled right down. That day was the beginning of us building a relationship of trust. Both of us are intense, anxious and highly sensitive individuals. Becoming partners required that we spend a great deal of time together learning to speak the same language.

I spent a lot of time teaching him tricks that he learned quickly. Amistadd enjoyed playing ball with me. I would place a kid's ball on a cone, stand on one side of it and say, "Amistadd play ball!" Right on cue, Amistadd would then knock the ball off the cone and land it right at my feet. We then advanced to me placing a bucket on a step-ladder platform with a ball placed on the top rung. I would say, "Amistadd, ball in the bucket!" He would promptly push the ball off the rung directly into the bucket. I was stunned with his ability to learn tricks.

I decided to test his cognitive abilities by increasing the difficulty of tricks. I drug out Don's saw horse bench and placed two cups on top. I put a pine cone under one cup and a baseball under the other. I then said, "Amistadd, find the ball" not expecting him to comprehend. You can imagine my surprise when he actually pushed the correct cup over, reached over the saw horse and picked the ball up from the ground with his mouth. The baseball was rather heavy so he quickly dropped it.

Amistadd liked the ball so he would continue to pick it up and drop it some more.

Amistadd seemed to really understand the game, "find the hidden ball." To make sure, I switched the ball and pine cone around several more times without letting him watch which cups I placed them under. Amistadd amazed me by finding the hidden ball time after time. I videotaped Amistadd doing his tricks for proof, not sure anyone would believe all this. Amistadd went on to learn how to weave cones on cue without a lead rope, follow the leader (me) without a lead rope plus several more tricks. I finally ran out of trick ideas so the rascal came up with some of his own.

Amistadd was quite the Houdini and showed me that he could unlatch gates. For a time, Amistadd and his sister, Eufalla shared the same area. We had a round pen set up in the center of their pasture. He was very clever and enjoyed playing tricks on others. One evening, Amistadd unlatched the round pen gate. He lured his sister into the round pen. He somehow managed to shove the gate shut and lock Eufalla inside. The following morning, we were surprised to see Eufalla in the round pen with the gate shut. She was less than thrilled about her overnight camp out. I could swear Amistadd was chuckling over this.

Amistadd continued to show us his marvelous sense of

humor. He also now considered me "his person." Receiving Amistadd's trust and loyalty was a wonderful, but hard-earned gift. In turn, I gave him my respect, trust and devotion. What Amistadd had needed most was someone who could be his special person. That someone needed to be a person who could believe in him and accept him for who he is.

During those tough years of training, I had to learn to face my fear, embrace it and carry on despite his powerful antics. Don found a tee shirt for me with the perfect John Wayne saying. It goes like this, "Courage means being scared to death, but saddling up anyway!" Becoming Amistadd's friend took looking deeply into myself. I hate to admit it, but Amistadd and I are a lot alike. We dislike change and we tend to react quickly before thinking and then escalate. I had to learn to stay calm no matter what because Amistadd mirrored my behavior. Amistadd was helping me become a better person!

Amistadd Goes Camping

By June 2015, Amistadd and I were ready to take the next step. That following spring, Don and I took Amistadd, Puddin, J and Bo (Border Collies) camping out at our remote property near the Gearhart wilderness. I didn't know what to expect from Amistadd especially since he hadn't done much traveling in a horse trailer. Amistadd's biggest adventure away from home had involved his trip to the fairgrounds with Marie.

Hoping for the best, Don and I loaded up the horses and dogs. Amistadd was off on his first camping trip adventure. Once we arrived, Amistadd settled right into his camp site (corral) and made himself right at home. He seemed exceptionally delighted when his hay bag showed up. Don and I took Amistadd & Puddin on several rides out in unfamiliar territory during the weekend. Amistadd was on high alert during our rides, but he was also well under control. He even took the lead down the trail a few times. We were especially impressed with Amistadd when several deer jumped out of the brush and he barely spooked. In fact, he seemed excited about exploring new country with us.

Amistadd enjoyed his camping trip.

Amistadd Makes Friends

Amistadd was now ready to be introduced to people and more chaos. Later on that spring, Don and I took Amistadd and Puddin on a day outing to the Lily Glen Equestrian park. Lily Glen is located in the mountains 30 miles west of our home near Howard Prairie. People from all over bring their horses, trailers, campers, tents and a lot of noise to the Lily Glen campground.

During our day ride, Amistadd was introduced to sights and sounds he had never seen or heard before. He got to experience unfamiliar horses, noisy children, dogs, camp fires and chaos in general. Amistadd took everything in stride. He seemed to especially enjoy meeting Grace, a little girl and Sassy, her pony. The little girl came up to pet Amistadd and he was very calm and gentle in her presence. He was also very mannerly around Sassy. Besides taking me on a nice trail ride, he proved to be Mr. Social.

By June 2015, Amistadd was close to being ready for his first endurance ride, but he hadn't experienced an adrenaline high horse camp yet. Before we entered Amistadd in his first endurance event it was important to find out whether or not he could handle the high energy of a competitive camp environment. We received a wonderful opportunity to find out.

Amistadd's new friends, Grace and Sassy

Amistadd Camps with The Champs

A friend told me that the 2015 World Championship Ride and Tie event was going to be held at Aspen Lake, just ten miles west of our home. I decided to visit the Ride and Tie camp site and meet with Chris Amaral, the manager a few days before the event started. I explained our situation to Chris and asked if we could camp with them. Chris said yes. In fact, he welcomed us with open arms as did the other competitors.

On June 27, 2015, Don and I loaded up Amistadd, Puddin, J and Bo and headed off to the Ride and Tie camp site. Amistadd is a habitual kind of guy who likes routine so "change" has not always been his favorite word. We were pleasantly surprised when Amistadd exceeded our expectations that weekend. In fact, he did a wonderful job adjusting to this exciting camp atmosphere. Amistadd experienced everything from a bicyclist charging close by his corral to a woman on a nearby bucking horse. Don stood guard near Amistadd during these fiascoes, but Amistadd nonchalantly looked at these invaders as though he might be thinking, "What's their problem?"

Amistadd seemed to enjoy his camping experience with the Ride and Tie group. He wasn't bothered what so ever by their shot gun start and rowdy cheering. Riders and horses went screaming out of camp in a whirl wind of wild energy and Amistadd just calmly watched them go by.

Dick Root & his mare, Alivia lead the Ride & Tie pack as Amistadd calmly looks on.

Camping with the Ride and Tie folks showed us that Amistadd was ready for the next step; an actual AERC Endurance ride event. (AERC stands for American Endurance Riding Conference and is the governing body of nationwide endurance riding events).

Amistadd was very happy and relaxed at the Ride & Tie event.

Amistadd's First Endurance Adventure

Bandit Springs, July 2015

We entered Amistadd and Puddin in the 25-mile Limited Distance endurance event at Bandit Springs. Their event was scheduled for Sunday. Warren Barr, a good friend and Crystal, his endurance horse were kind enough to go with us on a warm up ride on Saturday.

Amistadd seemed interested in his surroundings as we walked through the busy endurance camp. I was relieved that Amistadd seemed okay with all the people, squealing horses and camp chaos.

Photo by Elayne Barkley

Our Saturday morning walk was uneventful for the most part other than Amistadd crossed a deep creek bed like a hunter jumper. Fortunately, this big jump happened so fast that I didn't have time to do anything else but ride the horse! Over all, Amistadd handled the excitement of his first endurance ride camp quite well. After our 5-mile practice ride, we returned to camp. Just after we unsaddled an intense thunder and lightning storm hit. It's a good thing that Amistadd is originally from the Willamette valley and used to pelting rain. The storm didn't seem to bother Amistadd as long as we kept his feed bag full of hay.

Amistadd and his hay bag were drenched!

There were only eleven participants signed up for our Sunday event. We felt that starting Amistadd with fewer horses on Sunday would be less stressful for his first endurance experience rather than going out on Saturday with a crowd. It quit raining Sunday morning, but we had reservations about running horses on slick muddy trails.

Sunday Morning 25-Mile Start

It was Sunday morning and we were off on our 25-mile endurance event. Our start down a gravel road was good. Amistadd was under control and he went into a nice smooth trot for me. On the other hand, Puddin was a maniac. She hadn't done an endurance ride in two years and boy was she jazzed up. Puddin pranced and danced all over the place. Don tried to keep her down, but she was "Puddin the Jack Hammer!" Since Don wouldn't let Puddin go "fast forward" she shot up and down like a yoyo instead. Our three-mile trot down the road continued to go smoothly for Amistadd and me. It was however another matter when we turned onto a single-track trail.

The trail was a mess of deep greasy mud! Everyone was slipping and sliding all over the place! Amistadd was uneasy about his footing, but he kept himself under control. Describing these conditions as "tough going" is an understatement. To make things worse, Amistadd was wearing Easy Boots and they kept sticking in the mud and sliding off. Each time we had to get off and fix them, we got out of sync with our pace.

Our first loop was supposed to be fifteen miles.

Unfortunately, we missed a turn and unintentionally cut the trail. This got us back into the vet check too soon. (The veterinarian check point was back in camp). We had to back out and redo a trail section. Having to back track was psychologically tough on the horses plus it added an extra 3 miles to our course putting us further behind. As I've mentioned before, Amistadd is very habitual by nature and he did not want to leave camp and go back out the same way he had just come in.

Amistadd is a wonderful horse, but very bullheaded by nature. There was nothing and "I mean nothing" I could do to convince that horse that he needed to turn around and back track. He is very intelligent and back tracking just made no sense to him. Don finally had to grab our lead rope and tow us about 500 yards back down the road before Amistadd would go on his own. To make matters worse, my camel back hydration pack burst and dumped water down my back side. My saddle and lower extremities were drenched! That sure was a miserable sensation. The trail was muddier than ever especially after so many horses had tromped through the goo ahead of us. To make matters worse, Puddin wanted to race back into camp. She fought the bit and did some flying leaps through the mud and strained a muscle. The strain was mild, but her gait was off at the vet check. She got disqualified. Amistadd passed his vet check with flying colors, but he thought he was finished.

I had a choice to finish the last 10-mile loop alone or pull Amistadd out of competition. After giving it some deep thought, my logic told me to pull out. Amistadd was a rookie and it wasn't wise to continue on alone. On the other hand, my intuition told me not to give up. It didn't feel right to stop now especially after all the hard work it took for us to get here.

I questioned myself further and asked, "Was it right to pull him out just because I was uneasy? He was still fit to continue. Amistadd may have had a different take on the matter. Stopping and going for lunch was probably his preference, however, I knew better than to ask his opinion on that. Don said that he would support my decision either way. Working with a spirited horse like Amistadd had taught me to acknowledge my fear, but not let it get the best of me.

After giving it more thought, I declared, "We're going on by ourselves." "I believe we can make it!" My decision was definite! Don seemed apprehensive, but proud that I had the courage to go on with Amistadd alone. Don kept Amistadd and Puddin at the vet check while I dashed back to the trailer. He let the horses rest and eat hay. During their R and R, I slipped and slid down the muddy road to our trailer as fast as I could go without falling. Amistadd and I were now really behind so I needed to hurry. I wasted no time changing into dry riding breeches. In my rush, I threw wet clothing every which way.

Our Border Collies, J and Bo were glad to see me. No doubt they were disappointed when I ran out the door and commanded, "Stay! "I barely had enough time to grab a small can of grape juice for my cantle bag. My hydration pack was trashed. I should have filled up a canteen, but I was not thinking about anything other than the need to be brave and "hurry up." I sensed that Amistadd and I were about to embark on the adventure of a life time and how right I was!

Everyone else in our event had already left camp for their last ten- mile loop. Amistadd and I were slow to leave because one of his Easy Boots had fallen apart and we had to locate a spare. Don helped put our equipment back together. I stuffed my fear and refused to let it hinder me. I was determined to do everything I could to help my friend (this special horse) successfully complete his first endurance event.

Without looking back, my rookie horse and I took off. It was time to believe in my horse and myself. We started off with me on foot leading Amistadd down the trail. A few yards south of camp it dawned on me just how alone we were. Yes, we were indeed off on the adventure of a life time. It felt a bit daunting. If I had previously known what we were about to face, would I have really gone forward? Perhaps it's a good thing I didn't know. Maybe Amistadd knew?

Amistadd reluctantly walked along with me and hollered non-stop for his partner, Puddin. He made it clear that leaving Puddin behind was not a wise move. About 300 yards down the trail with camp out of site, I attempted to mount up. Amistadd said, "No way" and ran me in circles! I found a wide tree stump, got up on it and let Amistadd play, "Ring Around the Rosie" for about 5 minutes. I held on to his lead rope hoping he would wear himself out.

Amistadd ran 20 or more fast circles around the stump flinging me around in the process. I'm not sure how many times he actually twirled me around, but it was a lot! Amistadd finally got so dizzy that he stood still for a minute. Even though I was dizzy myself, I was able to make a flying leap on to the saddle and off we went. Amistadd went forward like the powerful war horse he is until we came to an intersection.

I became hesitant as to which way to go. At the same moment, a wild horse on a nearby ridge let out a piercing scream!

There are wild horses in the Ochoco mountains who hang out by Bandit Springs. When the wild stud screamed, Amistadd stopped dead in his tracks and refused to budge. I believed him to say, "There's an angry horse up there!" "Don't worry about him," I replied. "You're tougher." From his mannerisms, I could tell that Amistadd thought, "I don't want to find out and I'm going back!" Amistadd then firmly planted all four feet and refused to go forward. I hopped off and physically drug him a way down the trail.

I hoped I had chosen the right trail at the intersection. Amistadd probably thought, "I hope so, too, you crazy woman!" A short way down the trail, God blessed us with a fairy God mother who was walking her German Shepherd dog and also serving as a volunteer for a trail rider's group. I felt relieved to run into her. Up until that time, I wasn't certain we were going in the right direction. She assured me that we were and wished us well. She also added that other endurance riders had become confused at that same intersection. That made me feel a little better because I pride myself in paying close attention to the trail.

I found another stump and Amistadd proceeded to play, "Merry Go Round" some more. Rather than fight with him, I stepped off the stump, walked him down the trail a few feet further by foot and then quickly got back on him from the ground. I was in the saddle before he knew what was up. That surprised the boy. He then put his head up and said, "Okay, you win." I cued him to go and he went into a beautiful and powerful trot down the trail. I naively thought, "Wow, this is going to be a nice final ten-mile ride and it isn't going to take us long to get back." "Yay!"

Oops! Why did I say, "yay?" I celebrated way too soon. Right in the middle of a lovely long stride, one of Amistadd's Easy Boots came off again due to the mud. *Darn!* I had to hop off and fix it. Bless him. He let me put the boot back on. He also allowed me to mount up from another stump. We no sooner got into the groove when another Easy Boot came off. They were a nuisance to say the least. Amistadd had not yet allowed anyone to nail on a set of horse shoes, so he needed these cumbersome horse boots.

"Poor Amistadd," I thought, feeling sorry for him. We played leap frog with Easy Boots for the next 5 miles. He was patient and good about me dismounting, adjusting his Easy Boots, getting back on and moving forward time after time. At one trail junction, we completely lost an Easy Boot and I could not locate it. Fortunately, I had a spare. I vowed that sometime soon, we would find a way to get him shod with horse shoes and nails. Someone had hurt Amistadd in his past by trimming his feet too close to the blood line. Don could barely get him to behave long enough to trim his feet and shoeing him was still out of the question!

Amistadd and I finally worked our way down the trail that wound north again and back towards camp. All other horses and riders were far ahead of us. We were completely alone in these damp, muddy woods. Traveling through these beautiful pine forests and meadows felt surreal. I consoled myself by thinking about Amistadd and how far he had come along during the past few years. I smiled to myself when I thought, "he is behaving extremely well under these adverse circumstances." I'm sure that Amistadd had no clue why we were running around out in the wilderness by ourselves, yet he was willing to keep going for me. I felt very proud of Amistadd. After all, he had never been to this strange and unfamiliar place before nor did he have a map.

We were about halfway finished with our loop and traveling on a single-track trail uphill when all hell broke out! The purple clouds over head looked threatening. Then suddenly, they darkened to black! This ominous change happened fast! Within seconds the rains came. It was no gentle summer shower. We were assaulted! The rain pelted us so hard that we were drenched within seconds. It did not let up! At the same time that the flood gates opened, an antelope leaped out of the brush and streaked right past us.

Amistadd and I both jumped! Amistadd regained his control. At that very moment, I knew Amistadd was more than just a good horse. Amistadd was a GREAT horse! "YOU'RE THE KING OF ARABIANS!" I shouted against the howling wind. The rain continued to beat on us and then LIGHTNING STRUCK! It flashed and lit up the woods like a horror movie! The strike was less than 100 yards away from where we stood. Thunder ROARED right above our heads just a split second after the flash. We were right in the strike zone!

At that moment, I prayed to God for mercy. I asked Him to please let us finish this endurance ride before or if He had to take us home. More flashes! More thunder! More rain whipped us hard! I truly believed we would be struck by lightning before we got off that mountain. There was no place to run for cover. I knew that hanging out under trees for safety was more dangerous than being out in the open. I sure hoped the next bolt wouldn't pick us for its conductor. There was no smart choice but to hang in there and keep moving forward.

Amistadd looked like a big drowned rat! I wondered what I looked like? *Darn*! Once again, another Easy Boot came off. I hopped off and reset it as quickly as I could. We needed to keep moving and get off that mountain fast! Driven by gusty winds, the biting rain continued to smack us around! Another lightning bolt struck close by. Thunder exploded over the top of us. The boom was deafening! I prayed for strength. I thanked God that I wasn't alone. I was after all with Amistadd, my powerful friend and the King of Arabians. I kept my fear in check. I asked myself, "Who would get us out of this mess?" My answer was, "No one!" This was a harsh realization. Surviving this experience was our responsibility and only ours. "Dig deep, we can do this, Amistadd," I said. It was up to me to show him some confidence. I had to believe in that horse and mean it. Just as important, I had to believe in myself!

I led Amistadd to another stump to remount. He balked and pulled violently away. He refused to go near that stump. I urged him on, but no way was he going to let me lead him there. I was momentarily perplexed. "WHAT IS IT MAN?" I shouted above the ear-splitting thunder. I must have been getting pretty tired by then because it wasn't until I looked closer that I saw the danger. I glanced at the stump and saw large shards of broken glass carpeting the ground. "The work of target shooters," I assumed.

I marveled at Amistadd's keen sixth sense and told him, thank you. Lightning continued to streak across the ominous sky. Thunder continued to snarl at us and the rain slapped us around some more! Our world had become an angry place. I was anxious to get going. Finally, I spotted another stump about 25-yards up the trail. This time, Amistadd cooperated and let me get on.

Off we went again. We were both totally soaked to the bone by now. I asked myself, "Why on earth had I previously let a little leaky hydration pack bother me?" The adverse trail conditions worsened. Amistadd continued to move forward bravely. I was astonished that he continued to move forward with such treacherous footing. Because of the ever-deepening mud, Amistadd began to slow down. I tried to get him into a trot, but the poor guy kept slipping. I reminded Amistadd that we needed to get off the mountain before we got struck by lightning.

An Easy Boot slipped off again. "Oh, no!" I exclaimed. "Not again!" I slid off Amistadd's back and nearly fell flat on my "you know what!" The trail had now transformed into a big slip and slide. Hurrying seemed futile. I said, "Big man, you're doing great." "This is too tough." There was no longer any traction for him with those boots. I took off all four Easy Boots, but only two fit in the cantle bag. Thinking quickly, I tied the others to the saddle horn. I loosened his cinch to add some comfort, gulped down my little can of grape juice and offered Amistadd some carrots. Amistadd did not want any carrots. He looked discouraged. I figured that we had about 6 more miles to go. Walking even one more foot felt formidable under these conditions. I reached deep down inside for more energy and spoke to Amistadd with as much courage as I could muster. From that point on, we walked together with me on foot. I slipped and slid all over the trail right alongside of him. I quickly developed a great appreciation for what that guy had been doing for me.

I soon realized even more just how hard he had been working. It must have been pretty tricky just keeping me balanced on his back. WOW! What a tremendous amount of work it was just to keep from falling down. Amistadd impressed me. To gain traction, I led him off to the side of the trail through sage brush and grass whenever I could find some. We pressed forward up hills and down steep narrow slopes in a steady down pour. The endurance course trail was not a straight shot back to camp. It zigzagged back and forth in several places.

We must have been fairly close to camp once because, at one spot, Amistadd suddenly put on his horse shoe brakes. He batted me in the back with his head and shoved me in a different direction. He was indicating that we should go cross country back to camp. I tugged one way. He tugged back. I tugged some more and he batted me more. I kept doing my best to lead him down the trail. He kept shoving me around. Amistadd was pretty good at putting on his brakes in the mud. At least his brakes were working. I wasn't sure about mine.

Amistadd kept telling me we were going the wrong way. I knew he was right. The trail was moving away from camp not towards it, but to finish the event, we had to stay on the course. Amistadd kept communicating, "Camp is right over that hill!" Well, I might have gone in that direction and said, "to heck with finishing this ride course," had I known for sure that the cross-country route was passable. I was certain that camp was where Amistadd told me it was. I didn't know how treacherous the cross-country terrain was so there was no sense in taking the easy way out, "Sorry Amistadd." "No short cuts," I said. Amistadd reluctantly agreed to follow me away from the direction of camp.

We headed back down the slippery endurance trail. He continued to communicate that we were going the wrong way. At times, I was tempted to give in to his will and say, "Okay, let's forget about completing the course and risk going cross-country."

More than anything, I needed Amistadd to trust me even if I wasn't making any sense. Fortunately, he did trust me enough to quit playing tug of war. This was the moment, I realized having done all those ground work and trust building exercises had paid off.

The rain continued and we just kept moving. I refused to let myself think the word, "tired!" Instead, I kept chanting, "Amistadd, we can do it." This wasn't just rhetoric. I worked hard to put feeling into my words. It was my turn to encourage him. Once again, I thanked God for not allowing us to get struck by lightning. I was also thankful that Amistadd was willing to trust me and keep going against these odds.

We finally got off the mountain with both of us sliding all the way down on our back sides. Fortunately, we didn't collide with a tree, boulder or one another when we finally landed at the bottom together. Yay! We reached flat ground, regained our balance and onward we marched. I began to feel weary and then scolded myself for thinking those thoughts. I kept telling myself, "We can't quit!" "Who's going to come and get us anyway?"

No one knew where we were. We had to keep going. Then as quickly as it started, the rain quit and the sun came out. My spirits lifted. Consequently, so did Amistadd's. It seemed like we had been walking and sloshing through the mud for days. We still weren't heading in the direction of camp but at least the sun was out. I picked up our walking pace and said with enthusiasm, "Come on Amistadd!" "We've got to keep going." "You can do it."

By now I figured that we must be on some unknown trail heading towards who knows where. Due to all the rain, there were no more tracks to follow. There were wet marker ribbons here and there, but I became a bit delusional and wondered if we were following the right ones. I began doubting myself. For a moment, I wondered if we were still on the 10-mile loop or if we had missed a turn and crossed over to the 50-mile course. I had illusions of walking 25 or 50 more miles back to camp. I had no idea if we were still on the right trail loop or not. For the first time, true fear gripped my gut. Amistadd got nervous, too. I had to let go of my worry for his sake as well as my own.

I figured that this muddy excuse for a trail had to lead us somewhere so we might as well keep trudging along. Later on, Don and Warren said they thought they could hear me in the distance, just over the hill yelling out, "Come on Amistadd, you can do it," but we never showed up. They must have heard me when Amistadd was stubbornly playing mule and insisting that we go cross country. The trail into camp kept going in the opposite direction before it made a final switch back towards camp.

Warren and Crystal had made it back to camp about 30 minutes before we got there. Warren successfully vetted Crystal in and then joined Don to wait for me and Amistadd. Don was becoming concerned since we were the last ones out there and taking so long to get back. Finally, the trail veered west again and I felt confident that we were now heading in the direction of camp. Amistadd knew we were heading back to camp for real this time and he powered himself up. He tried to lead me a few times which made negotiating the mud even more interesting.

Somehow, we came to an agreement that I could still lead if I agreed to move my rear a little faster. We approached a wooden bridge on the trail. What a relief. I recognized the bridge. Amistadd saw the bridge and communicated, "That's a strange thing." Amistadd does not like strange things. I finally knew exactly where we were. I ignored Amistadd's antics as he suspiciously eyed the bridge. Camp had to be no further than a mile away. Amistadd spoke a little louder about NOT liking that bridge. I ignored him some more. It took a lot of coaxing to get him to approach the bridge. He snorted at it.

When I said, "Come on," he said, "Uh, no thank you!" I started to lead us on a detour around it. Then to my surprise and without warning, Amistadd sprinted across the bridge with me orbiting alongside. The good news is I didn't break my ankle. More good news; when we reached the other side, I still had a hold of his lead rope and my feet were on the ground. What a relief. We were past the bridge and there were no trolls under it. Then it dawned on me that Amistadd had flown across that bridge and I (not by choice) had taken the detour alone. I made a mental note to add bridge crossings to our future training exercises.

The trail veered south again. The camp was west and not south. Amistadd looked at me and balked again. I can't say that I blame him. He knew camp was west and not south. I am sure that by now, he was thinking, "My crazy person is lost again!" Really, who in their right mind would willingly go traipsing around in the wilderness only to be tormented by rain, mud, deafened by thunder and chased by lightning bolts?

Amistad and I had a few more hills to climb and then the trail turned due west without any more switch backs. Camp was less than 200 yards away. Amistadd knew it. If horses smile, he did. Amistadd was elated. His head and tail came up. Amistadd bowed his neck proudly and he was ready to trot. Well, I was still on the ground, but I thought, "Okay, why not trot alongside of him?" The trail was more firm and less muddy here. I don't know how I geared up, but I did and we both trotted into camp together at a fast and powerful pace.

Amistadd looked like a mighty fine Arabian war horse. As we trotted across the finish line together, my second wind kicked in and with a burst of energy, I exclaimed, "I'm so proud of you!" He sensed my pride in him and picked up his pace a notch or perhaps it was because he saw his corral and hay bag as we trotted on by to the vet station. At any rate, I remember thinking, "He's magnificent."

I could tell that Amistadd was really proud of himself. At some level, I'm sure he knew that he had accomplished something important. Amistadd is an intelligent horse. He knew that he had gotten his lost person back to safety. Don was there filming our first endurance finish. Warren was applauding. "We made it!" I exclaimed. Amistadd and I couldn't have done it without each other. Amistadd passed his vet examination with straight A's on his report card. Cassee Terry, veterinarian said, "Your rookie did a fine job." Well, Amistadd placed in the top ten in the most unusual way. He placed ninth, but there were only nine finishers. LOL! I had to chuckle at that one. Our atypical completion awards were a blue whiskey flask and a shot glass. I also had to laugh at that. After what Amistadd went through perhaps he would have liked a flask filled with hard core apple juice.

Really, I could have cared less about what award we got as long as we finished successfully. Even more important was Amistadd being in good shape at the finish and that he had a good time. Did Amistadd have a good time? I'm not sure about that, but I know I was extremely proud of him for completing such a tough event. One thing I know for sure; Amistadd was extremely happy to get back to his corral and hay bag.

Later on, I told Don that I thought the lightning probably struck close to us on top of the mountain. Don verified that it had. While we were up on the mountain, Don was back at camp, counting the blasts after each strike and calculating the time, distance and direction of each one. Don told me that he was sure the lightning strikes hit directly above us on the mountain. So, what did I learn from this adventure?

Well, I learned that it took both of us to make it through. It could have been a lonely trail out there battling the elements all by myself. Any number of times, Amistadd could have run off from me if he had really wanted to. It certainly pays to have a good relationship with your horse.

"Whew, taking care of my person sure is a lot of work!"

"Lord, I pray for strength to keep trying, to let no obstacle seem too great
for me, to keep saying, I can do it, I can make it!" -Amen-

Amistadd and April at the Bandit Springs Endurance Ride, July 2020

Photo by Kelsey Shane, "Out of Steam Photography"

Even though we are all senior citizens no one is quite ready for retirement yet. Amistadd age 23 and Samsarra (Samie) 22 successfully completed the 25-mile Mary and Anna Memorial Endurance ride in August of 2020. We are very proud of both horses. They showed us that one's age can be just a number as long as one has good health. Don and I are very careful not to over tax our horses and push them past their limits. Both Samie and Amistadd love to run, but we manage and pace them.

Both horses received all A' s on their final vet exam report cards. Considering their backgrounds and ages, this was a great accomplishment for them. Samie had been a throw-away endurance horse who others said would never amount to anything. Amistadd had been deeply troubled and you already know his background. The fact that they both successfully finished this event and had a good time is the best award we could ever receive. Amistadd met another milestone back in August of 2015. Don was able to nail horse shoes on him.

April, Amistadd, Don and Samie

Photo by Jala Neufield, Mary & Anna Memorial Ride,
August 2020

Chapter 6: Sir Richard

Richard with Jerry Depuy

Beating the Odds, Hard-Luck Horse Becomes a Champion

Article written by Marcia McGonigle, Herald and News 3/24/04

When Jerry Depuy first met Richard, the horse couldn't walk without help. "He was so weak, he couldn't stand by himself," Jerry said. (Richard was living with Jerry's son, Don and daughter-in-law, April at the time). "We didn't know if he would make it." "The vets had been talking about putting him down." Thanks to Don's good care, Richard began to recover.

Six years later Jerry Depuy, 64 and Richard, 6 began competing on the endurance riding circuit 25 to 30-mile rides through Central and Southern Oregon meant to test the mental and physical fitness of both rider and horse. In January, the two took home top honors at the Pacific Northwest Endurance Riding Conference (PNER), earning the Rookie Horse and Rider Award for 2003. The conference covers riders from British Columbia, Washington, Idaho, Montana and Oregon. Jerry accepted the award in front of 450 people.

The road to the award was full of hurdles. The first hurdle was Richard living. The second was convincing competition officials that Richard, a 16 hand, 1,400-pound warmblood, was physically able to finish the course. A warmblood is a mix of draft horse, thoroughbred and Arabian. Most people believe that such a big horse would have a tough time competing in long-distance races. He is the first warmblood to ever win a PNER Rookie Horse of the Year award.

Richard arrived at Jerry's home after his son, Don Depuy, talked his father into caring for the horse. Don Depuy works closely with the Klamath Humane Society, training their rescue horses and also taking in abused horses. Richard was taken from his original owner after the horse was found lying in his urine and feces and unable to stand or walk. His genitals were swollen. He was underfed and the veterinarians didn't expect him to recover. When Jerry Depuy met Richard, he wasn't sure what to think. Jerry was recovering from back surgery and had just retired from 23 years as a maintenance supervisor with the Klamath County School District. Nursing a horse back to health wasn't on his agenda, but he loved horses and had spent years on the rodeo and roping circuit.

Richard arrived in 1998, stumbling out of the horse trailer. For two months, Don Depuy gave Richard two shots of medicine a day to fight an infection. Jerry continued Richard's medical care when Richard went to live with him. "Jerry worked and worked with him," said his wife, Jo. "He probably looked in on Richard 50 times a day."

It took a year of constant work, but the time and effort paid off. Richard was big for his age. The family didn't realize that Richard was only 2 when they took him elk hunting. "Some horses you can't do anything with them because of the abuse," Jo said, "but he really took a liking to Jerry." "He's just an all-round horse," Jerry added. "He can do anything."

Jerry and Richard began training for the endurance riding circuit last spring after Don and April, his son and daughter-in-law, asked him to try it. Jerry and Jo Depuy had spent their retirement so far traveling and golfing, and both were ready to try something new. They bought a living quarters horse trailer and started planning for races, spacing out endurance rides at least three weeks apart.

Jerry began training Richard with long rides up and over Stukel Mountain, following a training program with help from Don. The horse and rider rode 50 to 100 practice miles a week to get in shape. Their first race was in May 2003. A horse's fitness level is important because during endurance races, the horses have to pass veterinarian checks. One of the requirements is that a horse's pulse rate be at 60 beats per minute within 15 minutes of arriving at the checkpoint. "Most of the time, they say a big horse like this doesn't have the ability to keep running that long," Jerry said.

At their first race, a 25-mile ride at Grizzly Mountain near Prineville, a veterinarian discouraged Jerry from competing, saying Richard was too big a horse to finish. Richard proved him wrong. Despite a rocky start-Richard bucked for the first 4.2 miles-the two did well, completing the ride and passing the vet check. It was the first of seven races for the duo.

Jerry and Richard both earned their Rookie of the Year awards for completing the most races. Jerry was named the top 10 Pacific N.W. Rookie rider for 2003 for completing the most miles during the season. His family made him a large belt buckle commemorating the award. Richard received a special horse blanket from the Pacific N.W. Endurance riding association.

Jerry said that racing with a large horse like Richard is simply a matter of pacing. He will slow Richard down as needed and also as they near veterinarian check points. Others may keep their horses moving quickly, but then must wait longer at the checkpoint for their horse's pulses to slow down.

The closest endurance event to Klamath Falls is the Pacific Crest Endurance ride. It starts at Lily Glen Equestrian camp and the trail goes on the Pacific Crest trail. The course requires horses and riders to climb 3,800 feet to 5,500 in the first 15 miles. At the top is a veterinarian checkpoint. "A lot of people who start out fast don't make it," Jerry explained. "You have to manage your horse

and the trail. It's more of a thinking game than a flat-out race."
One has a certain amount of time allowed for completing a ride.
Seven hours is allowed for a 30-mile event. Jerry and Richard
finished 11th out of 32 finishers at the Pacific Crest ride. Fifteen of
47 who started were disqualified at the veterinarian check points.
Jerry's goal isn't to win races, but for him and Richard to enjoy the
experience.

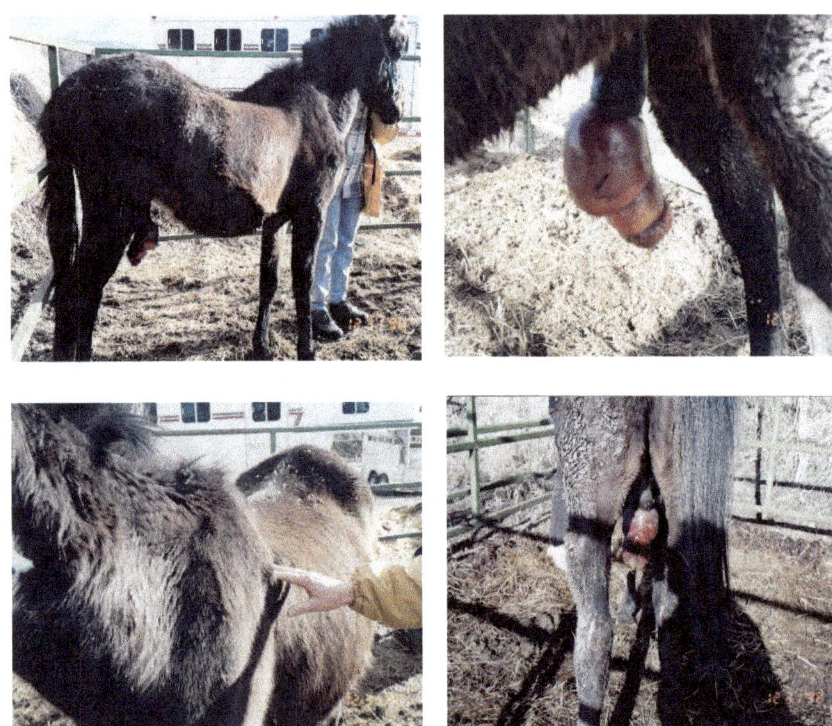

Richard was a yearling warmblood who was weak from
starvation. He was neglected and left to lay in his own urine and

feces. This caused a serious infection in his genitals. Charlotte Barks, Large Animal Humane Society manager and Nadine Hoy, Horse Rescuer, asked Don and April to assist them with Richard's rescue. Richard's condition was one of the worst we have ever seen. His recovery was miraculous.

Richard before recovery

Richard after recovery

Jerry and Richard at the Santiam Endurance ride, photo by Joyce Brown

Chapter 7: A Beautiful Horse

Don received a call from Sara, an Arabian horse breeder one day. She asked him if he would look at a troubled horse and possibly do something with her. Her name was Mahina and she was a highly bred Polish Arabian mare who Sara had bred and sold to some people.

Mahina was a sensitive and high-strung mare. The people

who bought Mahina tried to turn her into a Chariot racing horse. In addition, when they bred Mahina to their stallion, she got hung up in their homemade breeding box. The box broke. Mahina panicked and fled down the road in terror, dragging the box behind her.

Mahina had no reason to trust anyone. Other than being hooked up to a Chariot cart, Mahina had not received any other training. Mahina did not like being a Chariot horse nor did she enjoy being a brood mare. She had several nice foals for her owners, but they didn't like her. They found her difficult to deal with, called her names and kept her isolated in a pasture. Eventually they returned Mahina to Sara. Sara admitted that Mahina (Don renamed her Lonz) was untrained. Sara said that she didn't want Lonz because she had an overbite (buck teeth). Sara said, "I'm an artist and I can't have unattractive horses." Anyone who knows how we feel about horses can well imagine what was going through our minds when Sara said that.

Originally it was our understanding that Sara wanted us to train Lonz for her. WRONG! She wanted us to take Mahina (Lonz) off her hands. Being almost too kind-hearted, we agreed to take Lonz. What no one knew including Sara, is that Lonz had never been tied in a trailer. When Don went to tie Lonz in, she panicked, went over backwards and took Don's hand with her. This resulted in a broken hand for Don with 100 painful fractures. The pain was excruciating. Don, a man of many talents set his own hand. Don's hand eventually healed and he regained full use of it. That was another miracle that baffled doctors. Fortunately, Lonz was not hurt during the trailer mishap.

No one believed that Lonz would ever amount to anything. Don worked with her consistently. He got her broke and gained her trust and loyalty. Once she began to trust, she started showing us who she really was. Lonz was a sweet-spirited horse and an incredible athlete. She was a strong and fast runner. Don discovered that Lonz enjoyed running, so over the years, they participated in many endurance events together.

People in her past frequently told Lonz how ugly her teeth were. She had an inferiority complex and was ashamed of her teeth. So, you may wonder how we knew that. For one thing, Lonz refused to show her teeth to us. Don would have to pry her mouth open just to get a look at them. We made it a point to tell her how nice they were and how pretty she was. The reader may find this hard to believe, but Lonz understood what we were saying. After a while, she went out of her way to show us her teeth whenever we approached. She would clank them and grin. Don called it her "Clyde grin."

Horses certainly understand more than we think they do. I'm not sure if they read our thoughts, understand our words or both, but they seem to read us better than we do them. Perhaps God has given horses the gift of clairvoyance. At any rate, Lonz knew that we loved her. She was truly a beautiful horse!

Lonz and her beautiful smile!

Do we really understand beauty? Many Native American cultures viewed physical abnormalities as being something special. Someone with buck teeth, an exceptionally large nose, or some other abnormality was viewed as gifted, not cursed with ugliness. Perhaps if we considered one's unique distinctions as interesting, we would all feel better.

Lonz and the Box

During my school spring vacation (I was a Special Education teacher back then), I raked pine needles by the truck load. I decided to haul them out to the first horse pasture because Don had a good burn pile started out there. I also had 3 or 4 cardboard boxes that I thought would be good to add to the pile. I made sure that I buried the boxes deep within the pine needles so the wind couldn't blow them away and scare the horses.

Amistadd was temporarily camping out day and night in the round pen as part of his training program. Lonz and Whitey were free to roam around the pasture and around the perimeter of the round pen. Amistadd had recently been teasing and tormenting Lonz and Whitey unmercifully, which is the reason he got temporarily placed in time out.

The next morning after I had hauled 12 huge loads of pine needles out to the burn pile, Don observed a very interesting sight. He went outside around 5:15 a.m., a few minutes earlier than his usual time to feed horses. Lonz didn't know he was there watching. According to Don, Lonz actually walked over to the outside of the round pen with a box in her mouth. She sneaked up on Amistadd, who was fast asleep in the round pen.

Suddenly Lonz rattled the round pen bars up and down with the box. She did this several times with the intent to scare the "you know what" out of Amistadd. It worked!

Amistadd jumped several feet in the air, snorted and ran several laps around the round pen, terrified of the alien box attack upon his camp site. It didn't take much to stir Amistadd up, especially after being attacked by the wind and a flying wading pool a few days before. Don then witnessed something amazing. Lonz carried the box back to the burn pile, a good 25 feet away from the round pen. She then carefully put it back where she got it. I knew that Arabians were thinking animals, but this little incident really showed just how cunning and witty they can be. If it had been lighter outside, I'm sure Don would have seen Lonz raise her lip and show her Clyde grin.

Don and Lonz completed the 50-mile ride at the Klickitat Endurance event near Glenwood, Washington. We usually pace our endurance horses and don't allow them to run the entire course. We alternate between walking, trotting and perhaps some loping depending on the horse's physical condition at the time. Well, Lonz ran the last 25-miles of the 50-mile course because there was no way Don could hold her back. Fortunately, she was in great condition at the finish. Lonz was a phenomenal athlete and a great horse.

Don and Lonz at the finish line of the 50-mile Klickitat Endurance ride

Chapter 8: Eufalla, One Tough Little Horse

"You will not quit. You will keep up your brave performance because the very power of the eternal God surges deep within your being. O'God, may your power flow through me giving me the desire not only to get started, but to keep going!"

Photo by Dominique Cognee

We weren't looking for another horse when we met Eufalla. We stopped by Highland Arabians to visit a year after we purchased Amistadd. After showing us her horses and new foals, Robbin introduced us to Eufalla, a tiny yearling filly. Robbin shared that Eufalla had been raffled off for charity earlier that year. The people who won Eufalla divorced and returned Eufalla to Robbin the same year. Robbin went on to tell us that Eufalla was too small to do anything with. "Do you want her?" Robbin asked, without giving us time to say a word. Before we could answer, Robbin began shoving little Eufalla into the back of our trailer and said, "She's all yours!" Don and I were dumbfounded to say the least.

Maybe the words, "dumb dumbs" was stamped on our foreheads? Well, of course, Eufalla came home with us. She was exceptionally small, but we decided to work with her anyway. At two years old, Eufalla was still so tiny that Janica, our high school helper was the only one petite enough to ride Eufalla. Janica did a wonderful job helping Don train Eufalla and the two of them developed a close bond. Eufalla showed a zest for life and quickly became a good trail horse.

Although only 14 hands high, Eufalla showed a strong personality and a love for running. That short legged little thing could really pick those hooves up and put "em down fast." She ran with indescribable power; tail straight up and mane flying. Don jokingly nick named her "Our Cheer Leader." Eufalla finally grew, muscled up and we bigger people were able to ride her. Eufalla became my endurance horse.

Eufalla will be turning 19 years old this May 2021. She is still running strong and so far, has accrued 200 Endurance miles and 450 Limited Distance miles. This is amazing considering the trauma Eufalla has experienced in her past. Eufalla is a shorty, but she has shown the world that it isn't one's size that determines your strength and abilities. It's about one's heart, spirit, and determination.

"One's attitude determines one's altitude."

Quote by Pastor Randy Hadwick Photo by Joyce Brown, Oregon 100 Endurance event.

Shot Without a Gun

Janica Nowak is a special young lady and neighbor who has been helping us with our horses since age 13. She is now 21 and attends college in Idaho. During her college vacations, Janica returns to Southern Oregon to visit her family. She also continues to work with our horses.

This summer Don, my husband, hired Janica to help him train Amistadd, my Arabian gelding. Amistadd is a great horse, but is easily excitable so we got Janica suited up with a Kevlar protective vest and a helmet. She's got that bulletproof attitude that comes with youth.

Janica fearlessly approached her summer job with just a few stressful moments. Don and Janica worked diligently with Amistadd for three months. They survived intense lightning storms, sweltering heat and intense winds. They even encountered a black bear 50 feet from the trail who refused to move. Another day they faced a pack of coyotes and later on, bellowing range cattle. Through it all, Amistadd passed kindergarten and became a solid green broke horse.

Janica became an expert with taking a deep seat during some intense spooks and jumps, but never needed her Kevlar vest. Overall, Amistadd's summer training ended on a good note with no wrecks. We decided to invite Janica on a trail ride before she packed up and returned to college. Don suggested that we ride three of our well-trained mares so that we could all relax and enjoy the trail.

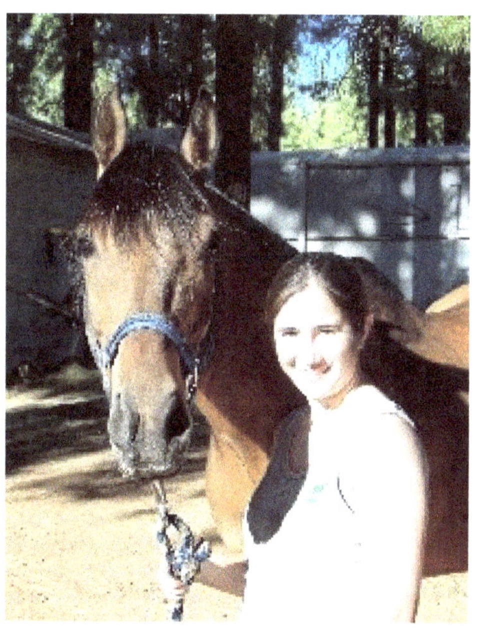

Janica and Amistadd

Janica chose to ride Eufalla on our so called "recreational" trail ride. I rode Puddin and Don was on Lonz. Janica rode without her protective vest, thinking, "I don't need it." "After all, I am just riding sweet little Eufalla." I didn't argue with her about wearing the protective vest. I did, however, insist that she wear her helmet.

We ride our horses throughout the rugged open range and timber country that borders our mountainous property in Southern Oregon. All three horses are veterans at navigating through rough terrain in all kinds of weather conditions ranging from extreme heat to deep snow. We've encountered all kinds of dangers during our many years of riding up here. Our horses have come face to face with a cougar, bear, elk, coyote, target shooters, ATV's, and horse eating boulders, but never anything like the following;

At 4:30 p.m. on Friday, August 12, 2010, we all mounted up. It was exceptionally hot, but we decided to ride anyway since Janica would soon be gone in just two days. Bo, our male Border Collie ran out to join us. His sister, J said, "Too hot" and hid under the porch. It's a good thing that she did. If J had been with us, I'm sure she would have high tailed it for home during the upcoming excitement.

Janica and I put on our helmets and Don grabbed his cowboy hat. You may wonder why no helmet for Don? Well, he is an authentic cowboy, ex-rancher and professional horse trainer. When younger, he rode the rodeo circuit. He learned to do a professional tuck and roll when riding bulls, saddle and bareback broncs. He says that his cowboy hat brim serves to break a fall. I think wearing a helmet when riding is a good idea, but each to his own. Janica and I wear helmets. We may roll, but sometimes forget to "tuck."

On this memorable Friday, we rode silently through some spectacular timber and canyon country. When riding, we do our best to focus on our horses. We usually ride quietly and seldom speak. We like to peacefully take in the natural beauty of our surroundings.

About 5 miles out, Bo appeared pretty hot so we decided to head towards a cattle reservoir where he could get a drink and swim. Bo took off for the pond. After a few minutes, Puddin and I rode closer to the reservoir to check on Bo. Just as I was encouraging Bo to go for a swim, Don yelled out that they were turning for home. He was about 25 yards from the pond when I heard him ask Janica to take the lead. I lingered a few seconds longer to let Bo finish his drink. The reservoir water was low this year so Bo got no more than a "Muddy Pond latte." What happened next sent shock waves through us all.

Janica and Eufalla turned east on a cow trail. Don and Lonz fell in behind them and I put Puddin into a trot to catch up. Bo took off after a squirrel rather than take up his usual position by the lead horse. Suddenly there was an explosion. The sound was deafening! All three horses jumped and Bo yelped! Don felt something slam hard up against his right hand. Eufalla bolted and my first thoughts were, "LAND MINES!"

Don thought my pistol had gone off, but he remembered that I didn't have it with me. He then spun around and looked towards the road thinking someone had just taken shots at us. His next thought was, "GRENADE!" At the same time, he knew he had actually seen the explosion, but still couldn't believe what he saw. The explosion originated from directly under Eufalla's foot. In fact, it actually bounced up from the ground, similar to a World War II land mine.

When the bullet cartridge exploded, Eufalla shot straight up in the air. She then hit the ground and stood still for a few seconds. By then, she must have realized her pain from the burning shrapnel. After standing still for a second or two, she bolted blindly through the sage brush. Eufalla bucked like a rodeo bronc all the way down the cow trail. Janica kept a deep seat in her good old 1903, a 110-year-old handmade western saddle.

Don guessed that Eufalla had to be running and bucking at speeds close to 20-25 mph. Janica kept her mind in the middle and was doing a fine job of riding her wild horse when suddenly Eufalla tripped over a rut. When Eufalla stumbled, Janica gave the mare her head and instinctively grabbed the lead rope. She was then thrown out of balance.

Before Janica could bale off, Eufalla took 3 major jumps and Janica was launched. None of us knew at the time that Eufalla was in major pain as she continued on with her bucking rage without her rider. Janica hit the ground hard. She landed on her back with a mighty WUMF! The impact cracked Janica's helmet all the way down the back, but it served its purpose and saved her from a traumatic head injury.

Later, Don remarked that even a pro couldn't have stayed with Eufalla at that point. "WOW, good job Janica!" "Cowgirl Down!" "Now Cowgirl Up!" This brave young lady had ridden the wild bucking bronc for at least 25 seconds. Don told me later that I proved I was capable of speaking at least 500-600 words per minute.

Eufalla was still running wildly due to the shrapnel that was cutting and burning the inside of her front legs. Anyone familiar with firearms can probably imagine just how painful hot shrapnel could be. Imagine what it might feel like having the inside of your calf cut with razor sharp shrapnel. We can't fault Eufalla for getting upset. Even a dead broke horse would have gotten shook up over this incident.

Don was ready to run Lonz down the trail to check on Janica when suddenly Eufalla doubled back at a full sprint, bucking, twisting and turning. She ran up the trail between Puddin and Lonz, and then right on past. Don was afraid that Eufalla would trample the girl if we ran our horses over to help.

I had one foot in the stirrup and the other half way out, waiting for Don to make a judgment call. With me standing with just one foot in the stirrup, he was afraid to run after Eufalla knowing that Puddin might bolt and unload me as well. Eufalla then surprised us and ran back up the trail and right over some more loaded cartridges. We were fortunate that these other shells didn't ignite. Later on, we found an entire pile of loaded bullets in the very same spot on the trail.

Lonz was still prancing and just a split second away from blowing up. Don dismounted and I handed Puddin over to him and took Lonz's lead rope. Don and Puddin ran Eufalla down. Eufalla stopped dead in her tracks when Puddin approached and Don called her name. I drug Lonz with me and ran to Janica as fast as I could. Janica was sitting on the ground among sage brush and dirt. She was in a daze and completely covered with dust.

I asked Janica to please talk to me. She looked up at me and asked, "What happened?" Janica didn't know why she was on the ground. I was holding Lonz, who continued to dance and squeal, plus was close to being out of control. Janica's eight years of experience as Don's apprentice instinctively kicked in. She immediately jumped up to help Lonz. This is what I believe brought Janica out of shock and back to reality. It took the two of us working together to hold Lonz down as she continued to twist, turn and scream.

Little did we know at the time that Lonz had been shot as well. By now, Eufalla had settled down some. Don led Eufalla and Puddin over to where I was standing with Janica and Lonz. He checked Janica out and also attempted to calm Lonz, who was still pretty wound up. Janica appeared physically okay other than she had some significant scratches on her back. Assured that Janica was okay, Don turned to Eufalla and discovered that her two front legs were cut and full of shrapnel, and also her chest near the cinch. Also, a small section of her right front hoof had been blown off.

Don checked Lonz over, too and saw that she also had cuts and shrapnel in her legs. The top part of Don's boot and toe had holes in them. Fortunately, he was wearing his Kevlar boots. He later dug some shrapnel out of his boots. If he hadn't been wearing those tough boots, we would have been digging shrapnel out of his legs as well.

Puddin had shrapnel lodged in her cinch, but it hadn't penetrated all the way, though. Bo was nervous, but A-okay, thanks to his squirrel hunting diversion during the explosion. Don shared his theory that Eufalla had stepped on a loaded gun cartridge. When Eufalla's horse shoe clipped the cartridge, the primer went off and shot us all. The next day, we returned to the scene. Don investigated and proved his theory to be correct.

Janica, who we first thought was okay, began repeating herself. She repetitively said the phrase, "I feel like I was in a dream." Janica is a highly intelligent young lady who is typically quiet and calm. She seldom speaks unless she has something meaningful to say or is encouraging someone. She certainly isn't in the habit of repeating herself. By the tenth time she repeated, "I feel like I've been in a dream," we realized that she was probably still in shock.

Don had Janica count his fingers. She could do that and also ask relevant questions about what just happened. Since she asked questions that made sense, we figured that she probably didn't have a concussion, but we weren't sure. Although she couldn't remember exactly what had happened, she knew where she currently was. She no longer appeared disoriented. Even so, we were still concerned about her and felt that she might be more seriously hurt than we thought. Don gave her water and suggested that we all move forward and start walking towards home.

Eufalla and Lonz were still wound up and hurting. Janica is a petite young lady, but like Eufalla she proves that you don't have to be large in stature to be tough and to do great things. She put her own pain aside and stepped forward to help her horse. Janica took Eufalla by the lead rope and started moving her out towards home. Eufalla tried to walk on Janica's feet. Perhaps she thought that was the safest place to be after the ground had attacked her.

Several times, we offered to take Janica's horse for her, but she wouldn't have it. She insisted on taking care of Eufalla herself. We walked about 3 miles, stopping every 200 yards or so to talk to Janica. We joked with her to help her relax. We checked her vital signs and tried to keep her talking and alert. Although she seemed physically well, she continued to repeat, "I feel like I've been in a dream!" Don and I explained to her several times what had just happened, but it didn't register. Evidently, Janica was continuing to experience some level of stress and trauma.

We all took turns talking to the animals, because they, too, appeared stressed. An hour later, we stopped for a longer break in the shade. I got into my cantle bag, found a water bottle and gave Bo some more to drink. The temperature by then was probably in the mid-nineties and everyone was hot and exhausted. People and animals all appeared a bit more relaxed and calmer after this brief rest in the shade. We asked Janica if she wanted to ride one of the other horses back now. She replied, "No, I still feel loopy and I need to walk." Don and I tried not to chuckle at her interesting choice of words. We had to admit that perhaps we both felt a bit "loopy" ourselves.

I continued to walk Puddin with me on foot so I could continue to check on Janica's well-being. About a mile further down the trail, she finally said, "I feel like the adrenalin has worn off." "What happened back there?" Janica had finally woken up completely. She then stated, "I don't feel loopy anymore." She insisted on riding Eufalla the rest of the way back home. I thought to myself, "Janica is a brave person."

Eufalla behaved like a perfect lady. She was amazingly calm and safely carried Janica back to our place. It dawned on me that by walking home calmly that Eufalla had already put the trauma behind her. I'm not sure that most horses could have done that under the same circumstances. Eufalla's bucking rage had been the result of shock, fear, and pain.

When we got home, everyone tied their horses to the hitching rail. I asked Janica to please sit down, but she insisted on unsaddling and taking care of her own horse. What a great young lady. She is probably one of the most responsible young people I have ever met. I made a quick trip into the house and brought back some juice and a damp cloth for Janica. She and I took a break while Don examined the horses further. He dug out more shrapnel from Eufalla and Lonz's legs. Fortunately, the wounds were superficial. He treated their wounds with iodine. Eufalla was going to require some corrective farrier work, but the hoof damage was not severe. Eufalla and Lonz were stiff and sore the next day, but were otherwise in pretty good shape.

A few days later, Don pulled shrapnel out of the top part of his boot. Fortunately, the shrapnel hadn't made it past the Kevlar fabric. Don's hand continued to sting so he grabbed a magnifying glass and discovered a small puncture wound. He dug out a small piece of brass and realized that his hand had been shot, too. Overall, he was no worse for wear. After resting for a bit, Janica appeared well recovered. She was quite amazed when we recounted the entire experience of being shot without a gun. She said that she remembered the explosion, but nothing else until she hit the ground.

 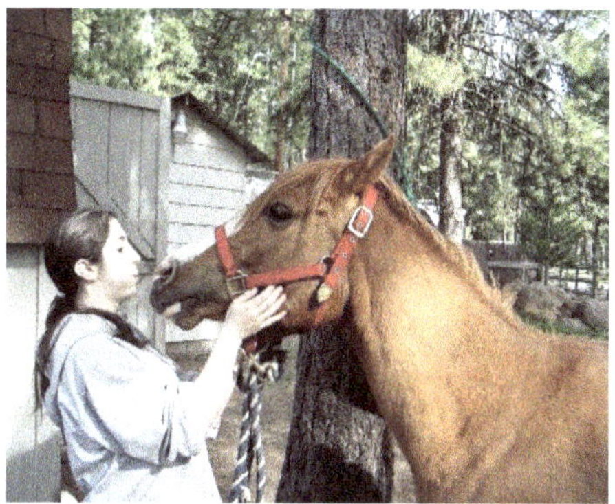

Janica and Eufalla, Two Toughies!

The next day, Don returned to the scene of the explosion. He found a handful of loaded 22 cartridge shells on the trail. They were old and some were partially buried in the hard-packed ground. He said we were fortunate that Eufalla clipped the ends of the cartridge with her horse shoe. Out of this handful, he discovered three bent cartridges. Don speculated that Eufalla had stepped on the rim of two or three of these loaded 22 cartridges and set off the primer of at least one.

If it had been a center fire cartridge, it would have been less likely to have gone off. As most people familiar with firearms probably know, a 22 cartridge is about the only one made with a primer around the perimeter instead of the center.

Was it fate or perhaps God's doing that this cartridge had been facing outward when it exploded? Others are welcome to believe whatever they wish, but the three of us believe that God helped us survive this extraordinary experience. If the cartridge had been pointing in the other direction, it would have exploded directly under Eufalla's foot. In that case, it is likely that her foot would have been completely blown off. What a horrifying thought!

After Don checked the tracks, he remarked, "Eufalla evidently ran over the loaded cartridges a second time when she doubled back." He stated, "It's a miracle that she didn't set off more cartridges." In addition, Lonz and Puddin had done quite a bit of dancing in the same place and it's a wonder they didn't set off another explosion.

All three horses, humans and one Border Collie survived this strange and unlikely experience. All three horses have moved past their Twilight Zone experience and are back to being happy and calm. I feel grateful that Don, Janica and I work well together as a team. Reflecting back, it sure paid off that we understood one another's signals and communicated with the horses in the same way. Janica instantly knew that I needed help with Lonz. She knew exactly what to say and do when helping the horses through this crisis. Janica is a great example of "Cowgirl Up!" She reached deep within, got herself off the ground and helped the horses through this crisis. She remained strong. It's amazing that she could get herself off the ground and help regain control of the horses during a confusing and frightening time.

After their wild experience, the horses were calm at home

We visited with Janica before she left for college. She reported feeling much better, although she was still a bit stiff and sore. I noticed that she already had her old bounce back. When Janica said goodbye for the summer, she smiled and said, "Well, I'll be back during my next summer break to help with the horses again." What a gutsy girl.

I hope this story helps you expect the unexpected at all times, especially for those who are around horses. As most of us know, under certain circumstances, even the best trained and well-mannered horse can be dangerous and unpredictable. Another mistake that most people make is believing that a 22 isn't as dangerous as other weapons. What many don't realize is that a 22 bullet can be extremely lethal up to a mile and a quarter. Don and I hope that people will remember to pick up any loaded cartridges that they drop.

A few days after this incident, Don and I were in town at the ranch store. I saw a tee-shirt that said it all. "Grab the reins of life and ride!" We bought it for Janica. If nothing else, this experience reminded all three of us that life throws out the unexpected. If you want to survive, what else can you do, but hang on to the reins tight, ride it out or tuck and roll. If you hit the ground get back up, help somebody else if you can and keep moving forward. Then chances are things will be okay.

Left: What could have happened.

Right: What did happen.

Eufalla, Toughie

The day after Don returned home from elk hunting (end of October 2016), Lonz contacted Pigeon fever, a dreaded horse disease. It is a horrible illness that impacts large animals such as horses, cows and sheep. It used to be called Dry Land Distemper, is caused by bacteria that lives in the ground and is highly contagious. It usually only resurfaces when the ground has been extra dry such as during drought years. The last 3 to 4 summers have been exceptionally dry in our area. The disease is transmitted by flies. There is no vaccine for Pigeon fever and nothing one can do to prevent their horses from getting it.

The disease causes huge painful abscesses to form such as on the horse's chest and other parts of the body. The abscess will cause the chest to swell up, resembling that of a pigeon's chest and therefore, that's how the disease got its name. Most horses only get one abscess. Some horses don't survive. Lonz had a huge painful abscess above her eye. Tragically, the abscess was so deep that she was going to lose her eye. Besides the abscess, Lonz had other old age issues and the Pigeon fever did her in. Dakota Woodard, our caring veterinarian, broke this sad news to us. Lonz had to be euthanized and we were devastated.

Dakota sent the culture into the lab. It came back positive for Pigeon fever. Several days later, Eufalla came down with it. Her head swelled up like someone with hydrocephalus and she had a huge bloody hole (abscess) under her throat. Don is usually calm and collected during emergencies, however, when he saw Eufalla, he came racing in the house and shouted, "WE'VE GOT TO CALL THE VET NOW!"

When I saw Eufalla my heart stopped for a second. I was horrified! During the course of two months, poor Eufalla developed 14 bloody abscesses all over her body. Her chances of survival were slim. Dakota said it was one of the worst cases of Pigeon fever he had ever seen.

This was a heart-wrenching experience for us all. To give you a perspective, when younger, Don worked as an ambulance medic. He said nothing he saw as a medic was as gruesome and sickening as what we saw when doctoring Eufalla's abscesses. Even though Eufalla's chances of survival were slight, we could not give up on her. Don and I took turns checking on her every two hours day and night for the next 2½ months. Dakota came out as often as he could, but he couldn't be here every day. Don and I took over Dakota's duties in his absence such as draining the abscesses ourselves.

Doctoring Eufalla was difficult. What we went through is beyond one's imagination, but we kept a positive attitude for her sake. She was fighting for her life. Dakota, an exceptional person and veterinarian said that dealing with Pigeon fever was even tough on him. I love Eufalla so I made myself hang in there and deal with the gore. Something good came out of this experience for me. I learned to get over my aversion and past an inability to deal with bloody things.

I saw horrid sights beyond one's worst nightmares. Eufalla's abscesses had to be dealt with day after day. Don and I got very little sleep during this time. I don't know how Don managed to hang in there and deal with his day job at the same time. Fortunately, he is a strong man and I am thankful that he was willing to go through this to help my horse. Unfortunately, Eufalla's painful abscesses grew slowly before they came to a head and could be lanced. She suffered greatly, but Eufalla is tough and never complained. I don't know how she stayed so strong. Eufalla is one tough little horse.

One day, a big abscess formed over Eufalla's jugular on her neck. I believe it was "Divine Intervention" that prompted me to call Dakota when I did. Later, I learned that the timing helped saved her life. Once again, I thank God for his guidance. Don was at work and I was home due to being retired. It was up to me to make judgment calls for Eufalla during the day.

Fortunately, I went with my instincts and called Dakota. He had recently moved to Oregon from New Mexico. He was a talented and caring vet. It is a miracle that Dakota moved here when he did. Not just any vet would have dropped what he was doing and rushed out to help Eufalla as many times as he did. Dakota arrived, took one look at Eufalla and said, "You will have to help me with emergency surgery, RIGHT NOW AND RIGHT HERE IN THE YARD! The urgency in Dakota's voice left me no room to waiver. As I held Eufalla, I somehow remained calm and steady while Dakota lanced the bloody abscess near her jugular. One slip of his scalpel and it would have been the end of her. Dakota needed me to be steady in order for him to perform this touchy procedure. He also needed Eufalla to be awake and not sway so giving her a pain killer was out of the question.

Dakota did an amazing job and I did stay calm. Eufalla was incredibly brave. Without a sedative, she somehow tolerated being cut across the neck without moving or crying out. How many of us could have done that! Eufalla held tough and that's how she got the nick name of "Toughie." The procedure was successful.

Our front yard looked like a bloody war zone. Over two pints of blood and infection came pouring out of the lanced abscess. I didn't pass out. Whenever I think about this, I thank God again and again for giving me the strength to assist Dakota, because I couldn't have handled this with my own strength alone. For months our place continued to look like a bloody slaughter yard as more abscesses came to a head, and had to be lanced and drained. Every night when Don got home from work, he drained abscesses as I assisted. We were nauseated most of the time, but we still had to maintain a positive attitude for Eufalla's sake. It was a true test of our commitment. Don walked down to Eufalla's horse shelter at 10:00 one night. J and Bo, our dogs and Striper, the barn cat followed him down there. After checking on Eufalla, Don turned his bucket upside down and sat on it. He was exhausted and just wanted to rest there for a few minutes. Don fell sound asleep and the next thing he knew it was midnight. The cat was laying on his feet and there was a dog sitting on each side of him. Eufalla was standing quietly behind him. There is no doubt in my mind that animals have great compassion for one another.

Eufalla's condition worsened. For several weeks she could barely walk. My job was to encourage her and get her to walk with me during the day. It got to a point where I had to drag Eufalla a few feet from her shelter to the water trough. Making her move had to be done to help force the abscesses to a head so they could be lanced. Forcing Eufalla to do something that painful was hard on me. I had to persevere with this difficult task otherwise, she wasn't going to make it.

By now the poor thing had abscesses under her throat, on her neck, her sides, down one leg, under both flanks and next to her personal parts. It's astounding that any animal could endure that much pain and survive, but Eufalla continued to show bravery during this entire nightmare. Eufalla must have understood that we were trying to help her because she allowed us to administer these painful procedures. We couldn't give Eufalla antibiotics until all abscesses came to a head and were lanced. If antibiotics are given too soon to Pigeon fever victims, the disease usually returns.

By January, it appeared that Eufalla wasn't going to make it. She was in immense pain and could barely move. She was weakening daily. Even though she still showed a small spark and will to live, Eufalla steadily went downhill, but we refused to give up on her until we had to. Eufalla showed us over and over again that she is one of the toughest horses in the world. She may be short, but that little thing is made of steel. Let me rephrase that; "Eufalla is tougher than steel." "She is made of titanium." Eufalla proved once again, that it isn't one's size that determines how tough you are; it's one heart, spirit and determination. Eufalla has true grit!

"Even more amazing than the wonders of nature are the powers of the spirit."

-Helen Keller-

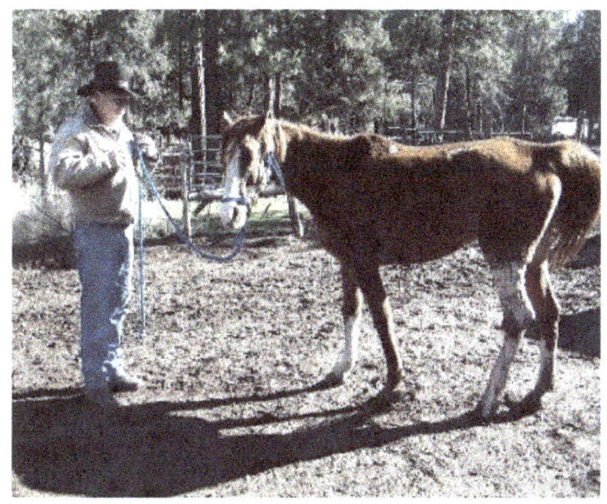
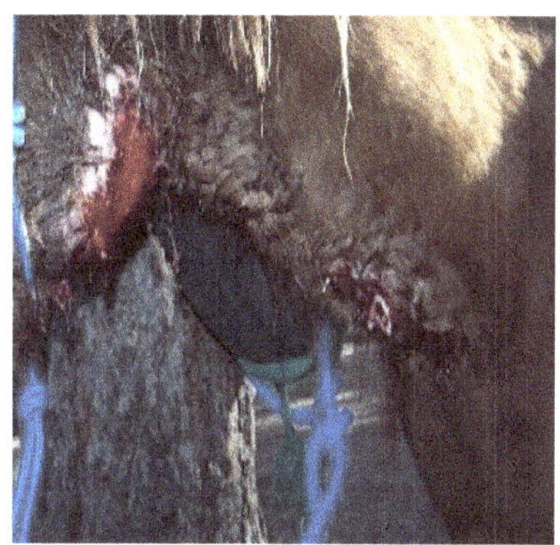

Eufalla with abscesses all over her body

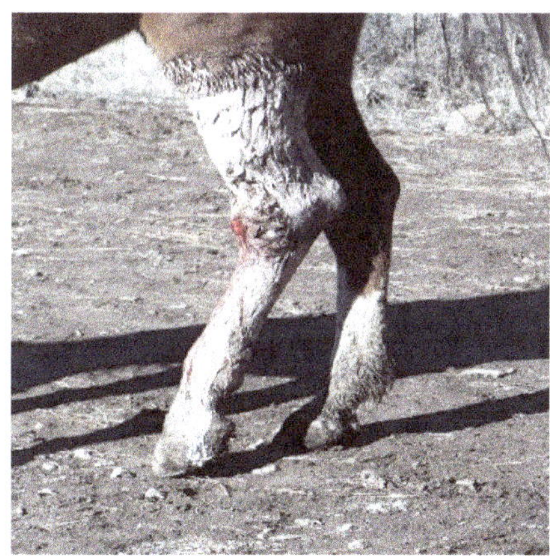
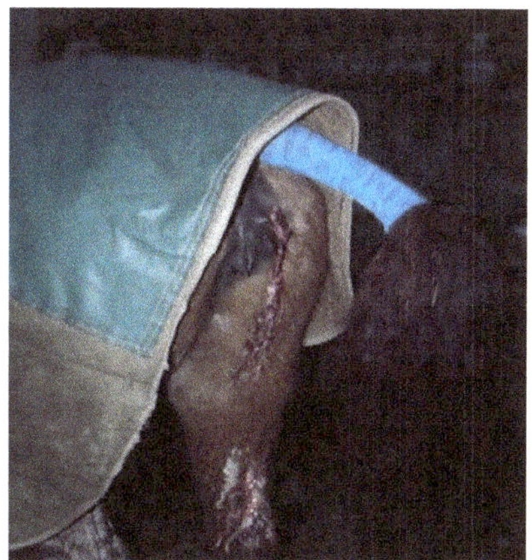

We continued to pray for Eufalla. Right when things looked darkest, light broke through hell. We will never forget the day Dakota lanced the last 3 abscesses. The amount of pain this caused Eufalla was unbelievable. Even though he gave Eufalla painkillers this time, she let down and cried mournfully for the first time. Her cries were heart wrenching. Every one of our horses showed empathy. They all lined up along their fences and starred at Eufalla with grave concern. When we led Eufalla back to her shelter, the other horses all hung their heads and were deathly quiet. I would swear I could see compassion in their eyes.

Everyone hurt for Eufalla, including the dogs and the cat. The amount of blood and infection shed on the ground this time made us all want to puke, including Dakota who is used to such a mess. Watching Dakota lance these last huge abscesses was one of the most difficult things I've witnessed in my entire 65 years. By now Eufalla was nothing but skin and bones. Slowly, but surely the antibiotics began to take effect. Eufalla began to improve daily and gain weight.

The abscesses began to heal and Eufalla was soon able to walk normally again. Although Eufalla was finally out of pain, she was still weak so I took her on short walks daily to build her strength. It wasn't long before she started showing her zest for life again. It was encouraging to hear her whinny when she saw us coming. It also did my heart good to see her beg for carrots and apples again.

She even felt well enough to buck and kick when Don went down to feed everyone.

Eufalla started getting well in the nick of time. Shortly after she started getting better; it snowed 3 feet. God is good! I don't know how we could have dealt with this Pigeon fever trauma with deep snow on the ground. We were blessed again. The bacteria that live in the ground were killed by the snowfall. The snow washed everything clean. Eufalla made a full recovery and went on to compete as an endurance horse the following year. As of 2024, Eufalla, "Miss Toughie" continues as a strong runner and athlete.

Eufalla in the lead at the Santiam Endurance Ride 2023

Photo by Jala Neufeld

Chapter 9: Dakota Woodard Special Person and Vet

Dakota James Woodard
Eufalla's Veterinarian and Special Friend

Dakota saved Eufalla's life. He also did a lot to help Don and me through this horrible Pigeon fever ordeal. He barely charged us anything for his visits. Most clinics charges would have been at least $300.00 per home visit. Dakota only charged us $100.00 per visit and sometimes nothing at all. Eufalla's antibiotics alone cost $2,000. If it weren't for Dakota, our total bill would have been well over $5,000. More important is the personal support that Dakota gave us. Besides being an excellent veterinarian, Dakota truly cared.

Dakota had prayed over Lonz when he put her to rest and brought Don a lock of her mane. Dakota's empathy for his patients and their owners was very sincere. He was also a real-life Dr. Doolittle. Dakota had a special way of connecting with animals and they loved him.

One day a doe and her fawn walked out of the woods and jumped over the fence. They stood right next to Dakota as he was putting on his mud boots and getting ready to treat Eufalla. The deer stopped just 3 feet from Dakota and appeared mesmerized by him. The doe and her fawn stood quietly right next to Dakota and watched him work on Eufalla the entire time. If I hadn't seen this with my own eyes, I wouldn't have believed it.

One wouldn't think Eufalla would show affection for someone causing her pain, but she openly showed affection for Dakota.

Each time when Dakota got ready to leave, Eufalla would try to pull away from me to follow him. Dakota passed away on January 17, 2020 from a tragic accident when his gun accidently went off. Dakota was only 31 years old. He and Kelsey were newlyweds. All who knew Dakota grieve his loss. It is hard to understand why such a wonderful young man had to leave us. The only thing I can figure out is that God needed him more than we do. "I pray that Dakota is now embarking on a new and beautiful journey." We will always be grateful for Dakota.

Dakota and Kelsey Woodard

Chapter 10: Spud's .04 Cent Check

Eighteen years ago, the Humane Society called and asked Don for advice regarding a sick horse. Spud, a big black quarter horse, was close to death. Druggies had abused him along with several other horses. They bought throw-away horses, misrepresented them and then sold them over the internet. These inhumane people were so abusive to animals that neighbors were finally able to gather enough proof to report them. Spud was just a youngster at the time and a mess. After being rescued, Humane Society workers discovered a huge splinter embedded in Spud's back right leg. The splinter caused a life-threatening infection. They had him checked out by a veterinarian who gave Spud little chance of surviving.

Spud required a shot and close monitoring every 4 hours. None of the Humane Society volunteers were able to stay at the shelter day and night to care for Spud. They asked us to please take Spud home for two weeks and provide his medical treatment. Don and I agreed. It was a rough winter here in Southern Oregon mountain country. We had three feet of snow and it had turned arctic cold. Caring for Spud was not going to be an easy task. We loaded reluctant Spud into our horse trailer and hauled the poor soul home. The mere 50-foot walk to our pasture was a struggle for Spud.

Don then trudged through deep snow every 4 hours night after night to give Spud his shot and to treat his ugly wound. The treatment was painful, but Spud was too sick to resist. His eyes were vacant and he appeared to have given up. One could see that Spud was in great pain. Honestly, neither Don nor I thought Spud was going to survive. No doubt about it, Spud was at death's door.

I remember looking out the window at this wretched creature and feeling heart sick. I read in the Bible that God cares about all of his creatures even the smallest sparrow, so I continued to pray for Spud. We didn't have shelter for him at the time. Poor Spud stood out in brutal cold elements with his head hanging low and dripping trails of blood in the pure white snow. Spud became listless and his future appeared dismal. Don never let up with his round-the-clock care despite Spud's slim chance of making it. Don consistently drug himself out of bed, giving his all to this mission.

Even though we tried to be hopeful, all indications showed that Spud was a goner. This miserable situation drug on for two more weeks, but we continued to pray anyway. Then miraculously, Spud turned the corner one day. Don went out one morning to check on Spud, expecting him to be dead. You can imagine Don's surprise when he spotted Spud walking about with his head up. He appeared alert and interested in his surroundings. Spud then continued to make amazing progress. Spud recovered completely within a month.

When we reported Spud's miraculous recovery to the Humane Society, they pleaded with us to adopt him. We already had 5 horses at the time and didn't need more. We prayed about it and then felt strongly that we were indeed supposed to adopt Spud. The Humane Society wanted $200.00 for Spud's adoption fee. This was discouraging news because we had some pressing bills at the time. We had also spent a lot on Spud's medical care. I asked God what he wanted us to do. I felt God's quiet voice urging us to go forward with the adoption. On blind faith, we made a commitment to adopt Spud and pay the $200.00. We had to do the right thing even if finances were tight that month.

Don and I had faith that we would figure out a way to pay those extra bills. Then another miracle happened! I received an unexpected gas mileage reimbursement check from my employers just a few days later. The check was for $199.96. WOW! That was enough money to cover Spud's adoption fee, lacking just a few cents. I knew this was an answer to prayer and a reminder that God is real and prayer is powerful! I thanked God for the check and then jokingly said, "Hey, God, how come you shorted me .04 cents?" "Ha ha" LOL!

Obviously, God has a sense of humor, too. You can imagine my shock when a few days later, I received a reimbursement check from a catalog company for exactly .04 cents! Unbelievable! Who sends anybody a check for just .04 cents?

How could this not be God's doing. The .04 cent check proved to me that God cares about both the big and small things in our lives. He does listen to us and He is always there.

A lesson learned; "Be sure to pray and have faith, but also remember to lighten up and laugh with God." "Doing the right thing can even be fun." Spud never became rideable, but he has enjoyed being a good pack horse. God loves all of His creatures. God loves Spud. He loves all of us.

Spud

SAVE 35-70%

ON OUTDOOR CLOTHING & EQUIPMENT
- FAMOUS NAME BRANDS -

SIERRA
TRADING POST®

6025 CAMPSTOOL ROAD • CHEYENNE, WY 82007

PHONE: 800-713-4534 FAX: 307-775-8054
www.SierraTradingPost.com

Customer # 5540689
Order # 11336113

Date : 03/30/06

DONALD & APRIL DEPUY
8706 BIG PINE WAY
KLAMATH FALLS, OR 97601-9074

Dear DONALD & APRIL DEPUY,

We have processed your order and the following item(s) were unavailable:

ITEM #............. DESCRIPTION................... QTY PRICE..
n/a   n/a   n/a n/a

Please find the attached refund check to include the amount of merchandise,
applicable shipping and tax associated with this order.

We apologize for any inconvenience this may have caused. We appreciate
your business and hope to hear from you soon.

Sincerely,

The Staff of SIERRA TRADING POST

Total Refund   0.04

SIERRA
TRADING POST®

6025 CAMPSTOOL ROAD CHEYENNE, WY 82007

U.S. Bank
3030 Corte Avenue · Ph. 634-2700
Cheyenne, WY 82007

Check Number 574109

Pay 0 dollars & FOUR cents

DATE   AMOUNT
03/30/06   0.04

Pay To
The
Order
of
Customer # 5540689
APRIL DEPUY
8706 BIG PINE WAY
KLAMATH FALLS, OR 97601-9074

⑆307070115⑆ 121269068866⑈

Spud's .04 cent check

Don and Spud get ready for a pack trip

Chapter 11: Joker

Joker is a quarter horse gelding who Don was training for a woman. This woman ended up having to sell Joker. She sold him to Linda, a young lady who lives in town. Linda boarded Joker at a stable and hired Don to help her work with Joker. The boarding facility continuously put Joker on green grass, causing him to develop the beginning stages of founder. Don and Linda were both concerned for Joker's well-being, so Don offered to board Joker at our place for a summer. Linda also wanted trail riding lessons so it was a good deal for them both. Don put Joker on a healthy diet and Joker's founder issues improved.

At the end of the summer, Linda moved Joker back to the boarding stables. Joker broke out twice and headed the 15 miles back towards our place. Each time, Linda found Joker running along the highway and was grateful that Joker wasn't miraculously hit and killed. Joker made it obvious that he did not like his boarding arrangements at the stables. Don and I talked it over and offered to board Joker year-round. During the next 7 years, Joker appeared happy here and made himself right at home.

During that time, Don and Linda worked with Joker and he became a great trail horse. Linda, a busy young mother, came out and rode Joker whenever she could. She was gracious and allowed other people we trusted to ride and exercise Joker. Joker did a lot to help others during the time he lived with us. Joker and Don helped Charlie, an Army vet with PTSD, learn to work with horses. Joker did a lot to help Charlie build confidence. Linda eventually moved Joker back to town to another stables and closer to where she lives. She is able to see Joker much more often now. We miss Joker, but from what we hear, Joker is in a good place.

Charlie and Joker on a trail ride

Top left photo: Linda & Joker are out on a trail ride with Don and Sinbad.

Top right photo: Linda is spending some quality time with Joker. Bottom left photo: Charlie practices riding with Joker.

Bottom right photo: Joker tells Charlie to stop, relax and take time to smell the flowers.

Chapter 12: Red

Janica Nowak and Red

Red was an elderly Paso Fino/Arabian mare. She was purchased by John Depuy, Don's uncle. John wanted a trail horse and Red was a good one. After a year, John needed to re-home Red for personal reasons. In addition, Red was going downhill. Don was in the hospital recovering from a broken leg, the result of a serious horse accident. Don had been training a stallion that slipped in the mud and fell on him, crushing his leg. While Don was delirious in the hospital, I asked him if we could take Red in and he said, "yes." Don did not recall that conversation later on, however, Red found a good home with us.

Red was older than the hills, but she loved to go. Red was in poor condition when she first arrived. She seemed to be happy here. Red gained weight and developed a new lease on life. She had a comfortable Paso Fino gait and she moved beautifully.

Janica Nowak, the young girl we mentored, adored Red and rode her often. Janica and Red successfully completed the Pacific Crest Endurance ride. Red and I completed the Dunes Endurance and the Prineville Endurance rides. The vets were impressed that an old horse in her thirties could do so well. Red loved to go and to be with us. She lived with us for 4 years and then passed away due to old age. Red was a great horse. Even though her time was short, she blessed us and hopefully, we did the same for her.

Top left: Red was in poor condition when she first arrived. We helped Red acquire a new lease on life.

Top right: Red and Janica at the Pacific Crest Endurance ride camp.

Lower left: Janica and Red competing in the 25-mile endurance event at Pacific Crest.

Lower right: April and Red at the Prineville Endurance ride 25-mile event.

Chapter 13: Sinbad Streak

Jerry Depuy, Don's dad bought Sinbad Streak when Sinbad was 5 years old and unbroke. Jerry called him Simmer. Sinbad was a kind and sweet-spirited gelding, but very headstrong with a tremendous amount of energy. Don helped his father train Sinbad for endurance. I assisted with Sinbad's endurance training as well. Sinbad was a handful, but in a good way.

Don successfully got Sinbad through the Pacific Crest Endurance ride, but it was definitely a workout. Sinbad and I completed the Rogue River and Santiam Cascade Endurance events. Sinbad buck jumped for 2 or 3 miles at the Santiam ride, but he finished his 50-mile event with flying colors. The vet said that Sinbad was fit to go another 50-miles that same day. Sinbad was magnificent. He was a strong runner and he loved it.

Jerry did some endurance events with Sinbad until he quit competing. Sinbad then became Jerry's elk hunting horse. After a few years, Jerry decided to quit riding altogether. Sinbad became bored so Don and I brought him out to our place. He lived with us for 3 years before he sadly passed away due to colic and a tumor. We still grieve his loss.

Don and Sinbad at the Bandit Springs Ride

Photo by Joyce Brown

Chapter 14: Two Amazing Rescues

Photo by Dominique Cognee

Samsarra (Samie) came to us as a very sensitive and beautiful, but fearful horse. She is a highly bred Arabian mare (Aur Samarix FV Farrubi) who had been re-homed a number of times in her past. Although athletic, Samie had not been successful as an endurance horse. Most recently, we acquired her from a friend who became fearful after an accident with Samsarra (not the horse's fault). We didn't need another horse, but rescuing Samie felt like the right thing to do. Little did we know that she would someday rescue us.

Despite Samie's nervousness, Don believed in her. She made progress. A year later, Don entered her in a Limited Distance endurance event. Samie did well and seemed to enjoy herself. This is a horse who others said would never amount to anything. Don entered her in a 50-mile event. Once again, she did well. We were very happy that she was becoming more confident. More important was knowing she now trusted and was connecting with Don. Still, Samsarra spooked when we encountered such things as wildlife, hikers and garbage. Don continued to display patience with her.

One day, a jack rabbit ran across the trail in front of us. As a confidence builder, Don called out, "Samie, chase the rabbit!" One can imagine his surprise when Samie gleefully took off after the rabbit. She enjoyed the chase. From that time on, Don and Samie have enjoyed the game of "chase the rabbit!" She showed an eagerness to chase anything that moved. No matter what they were chasing, squirrels, rabbits, or deer, this chase game enabled Samie to overcome her fear. Last summer, five years after we rescued Samsarra, she gave us the greatest payback ever.

We were out riding next to our home on Green Diamond private timber lands. Kaitlyn, an eighteen-year-old girl whom we were mentoring, was with us. A friend, Kelly, was also riding one of our horses. I was riding Amistadd just ahead of those two. Don and Samie were in the lead. It was about 9:45 a.m., not a time of the morning when we usually saw much wildlife. Suddenly, Samie halted and came to attention. Don glanced in the direction she was focused and saw a long tail sticking out of a manzanita bush less than four feet from us.

Don, a steady man during emergencies, shouted out, "CHASE THE RABBIT!" and Samie bravely did so. She charged a cougar estimated to be at least 180 pounds. Fearing for its life, the cougar leaped out of the brush and high tailed it out of there. Samie continued her charge until Don turned her back. The rest of us were stunned! Don's quick thinking and Samie's bravery saved us from a cougar attack. Later, back home, I'm sure that Samie told the other horses that she saw the biggest rabbit in the country.

Samie loves and trusts Don. The feeling is mutual. Taking enough time to build trust and respect with a horse is well worth the hard work and time commitment that it takes. We may have initially rescued Samsarra, but in the end, she rescued us. God bless that horse!

Don and Samie at the Mary and Anna Memorial Ride

Photo by Jala Neufield

Samie Chases Another Cougar

Over the years, Samsarra (Samie) has become an exceptional endurance runner and a very confident horse. She heroically saved Don from a second cougar attack during the fall of 2020, four years after the first time she rescued us. Don was riding Samie out in the woods by himself when they spooked a cougar in the brush. Before Don could say, "chase the rabbit," Samie took off after the cougar on her own at break neck speeds. Don said he didn't know a horse could run that fast. He held on for all he was worth as Samie chased the cougar for a mile, caught up to it and bit the tip of its tail. The cougar let out a YOWL and took off in terror for parts unknown. After the cougar ran up a rock cliff and out of sight, Samie calmed right down and appeared quite proud of herself.

Chapter 15: Paco, Home Sweet Home

Pacorro (Paco), an Arabian gelding, was rescued by the Humane Society when he was approximately 6 years old. He had been part of a large herd of purebred Arabian horses. His owners got into some kind of trouble, took off with 12 of their horses and abandoned 10 of them. Paco and the other 9 were left without food and water for several weeks. After being rescued, Paco lived at the Humane Society's Large Animal shelter for 3 years before being adopted.

Finally, someone adopted Paco, but they returned him a few months later. He then lived at the Humane Society for approximately 2 more years before being adopted out again. His next owners didn't understand him either and he was returned to the shelter once again. In good faith, the Humane Society then hired someone to professionally train Paco. Unknown to them, this trainer happened to be extremely rough on horses. He used spurs abusively and created new issues and problem for Paco. We figured that Paco had been misunderstood long enough. We adopted him and Don went to work to rebuild Paco's trust in people. It took 10 years of hard work, but Paco finally left his troubled past behind and now trusts Don completely. He knows he finally has a home!

After further training, Paco developed a love for running and became a good endurance horse.

Paco & Don take the lead at the Pacific Crest Endurance Ride
Photo by Dominique Cognee 2024

Don and Paco at the Mary & Anna Memorial Endurance Ride

Photo by Jala Neufeld, May 25, 2024.

Paco says, "Maybe they thought I was a camel?"

Don told me I'm a horse!

Chapter 16: K-2, The Ranch Horse Comes Home

July 25, 2020

K-2 is a ranch horse that we helped rescue from hell on May 20, 2020. Don and I, plus ten other volunteers, were involved with this rescue. In addition, there were 5 sheriffs, a Humane Society representative and a brand inspector on this mission. We all went east of Bonanza, Oregon to Langel Valley, where we witnessed one of the worst cases of animal abuse I've seen. A demonic woman had collected 40 animals which included cows, sheep, goats and 16 horses. She was intentionally starving them so they would die and she could then sell their body parts overseas. There must be a special spot in hell reserved for this woman.

The animals received no food or water for almost 2 months. By the time we arrived, half of them had died. We saw stacks of withered animal carcasses all over her place. The stench of death was horrific. It was all we could do to keep from vomiting as we helped rescue the remaining cows, sheep, goats and horses. All animals were bone-thin and could barely move. This woman had plenty of hay bales stacked just outside the animal's pens. These starving animals got to see food, but were not able to reach it. This cruelty added insult to insult. Only 8 of the 16 horses had survived this nightmare. K-2 was one of them. Like all the others, he was weak.

When Don loaded K-2 in the rescue trailer, K-2 could barely lift his head off the ground. Don had to basically lift and shove K-2 into a trailer. In fact, all the cows, goats, sheep and horses were so weak that it took several people to help lift and shove them into trailers.

I had a bucket of grain. I will never forget three bone-thin Jersey cows who looked longingly at me and the grain as I walked by their pen. I turned back and fed them the grain. One stopped, looked at me and touched my hand gently before I fed her more. Tears welled up in my eyes. I will never forget that Jersey cow's touch of gratitude. My heart hurt that day. These 3 Jersey cows eventually made it and ended up in a good home.

K-2 and 3 skinny mares, all from this same rescue, have been living out at the Klamath Large Animal shelter (Humane Society) now for almost three months. They are all quarter horses. They were so thin that it was debatable as to whether or not any of them would survive.

K-2 is the center horse, May 20, 2020, a few days after rescue

Laurie Finch, barn manager and Charlotte Barks, supervisor, are both amazing women. They have been working hard to rehabilitate these horses and have had much success. All 4 of these horses are going to make it and Terry Bloomfield, the veterinarian gave them all a clean bill of health. K-2 has two ranch brands. He was once a hard-working ranch horse who was probably once treated well by cowboys.

K-2 likes people, is friendly, and appears to know a lot. Don has been working with K-2 and the others out at the shelter on a weekly basis. K-2 always comes up and puts his head over the fence when he sees Don coming. He likes Don and his cowboy hat.

It is as though K-2 is looking for the cowboy he once used to have. Each week, K-2 follows Don around like a loyal dog. When we leave the shelter, K-2 always follows Don until the fence stops him. He stands at the fence and watches us until we are out of sight. He communicates his desire to go home with us loud and clear. Fortunately, our boarder horse moved out in April. We had room for one more. We were not planning on getting another horse, but some things are just meant to be. K-2, the cow horse, found his long-lost cowboy. K-2 came home with us last night, July 25, 2020. He immediately made himself right at home.

Because of his brand, Don had been calling him K-2 and the name stuck. Interestingly enough, K-2 instantly changed his demeanor when he arrived at our place. I guess he sensed he was in a good place where horses are cared for. He stood up straight and tall, lifted his head up high and showed us that he knew he was finally home!

K-2 was estimated to be over 20 years old when we brought him home. We figured he had worked hard most of his life as a cow horse and deserved to spend the last few years of his life in peace. When K-2 first arrived, he had difficulty walking. Don discovered that he had several abscesses in his feet. Don cleaned them out and did some corrective farrier work. Within a few months, K-2 began walking normally. In fact, he began racing around his pasture with Puddin and Samie, his 2 roommates.

Don also discovered that he was much younger than 20 and estimated his true age to be somewhere between 12 and 15. Our guess is that he was originally re-homed due to his abscesses that caused lameness. He is now fit as a fiddle. Puddin, the boss mare, loves him. In the past, Puddin always remained aloof around geldings. The funny thing is Puddin immediately drew close to K-2. They spend much of their time standing or running together. Perhaps their bond stems from Puddin's own understanding of what it's like to go without food and water.

K-2 waiting for his cowboy

K-2 found his cowboy and a good home (K-2 on the left & Puddin on the right)

Chapter 17: Dreamer, A Story Yet to Unfold

Dreamer at 6 months old on rescue day

Dreamer was discovered at the auction yard by a Humane Society volunteer who rescued and purchased her for $45.00 and then brought her out to the shelter in the fall of 2019. She was malnourished and just 6 or 8 months old. Don and I worked with her at the shelter for about a year before adopting her. Dreamer, an Anglo/Arab, was a pathetic bag of bones and an ugly duckling. She has always been large for her age. We decided to adopt Dreamer because we felt she would be misunderstood due to her large size, but young age. We brought her home on February 17, 2019. She now stands close to 17 hands high and is gorgeous. Dreamer is kind, strong and athletic. She is our special girl! Dreamer truly is the ugly duckling who turned into a beautiful swan.

Dreamer in training 2023

Dreamer and April are ready to ride the trails & miles 2024

Dreamer

"My strength is as the strength of ten because my heart is pure"

Chapter 18: A Beautiful Thing

April 20, 2015

This morning, my 53rd birthday, I walked outside to start my car for work. It was cold, overcast, and drizzly. After I started my car, I called Bobby dog and said, "Let's go for a walk." I saw a sudden movement so I glanced across the cul-de-sac and saw a beautiful thing. A crippled doe struggled to cross the cul-de-sac with her fawn. I watched her limp and almost fall to the ground as she took each stride, but she got up anyway and kept going on. Although her movements were slow and laborious, she made it safely across the road and back into the woods with her fawn, who bounced on ahead of her.

I called out to her and with much respect, I said, "You're sure a tough old girl." She paused and looked at me, possibly recognizing my voice tone as one of encouragement and approval. You might be wondering how this could possibly be a beautiful thing. Well, a year ago, this doe was hit by a reckless driver in our neighborhood. The doe's leg was broken, yet she struggled to get up anyway. Don and I thought she would soon die or be killed by predators.

We stood out on the back porch watching her. Don wondered out loud if he should shoot her and put her out of her misery. Each time we looked at her, she stared back with eyes that showed an unbelievable strength of character. She didn't try to flee or give up but just continued to carry on despite her pain. We sadly watched her struggle as she limped behind the other deer. We were amazed that she didn't give up. She would fall right in behind the deer herd and keep right on going. We thought she would be left behind, but she struggled to keep up anyway. We watched her move forward until she finally disappeared into the brush behind the others.

We didn't think we would see her again. You can imagine our surprise when we saw the old girl a few days later. She continued on with her broken leg. She trailed behind the herd day after day for about two weeks. It was obvious that this animal was in immense pain. We could feel it. Don announced that he couldn't stand it any longer. He stated that he would shoot the doe and put her out of her misery. I felt sad, but knew this had to be done. It was indeed the kind thing to do. I tried to put this sad situation out of my mind the best that I could.

Several weeks later, I looked out the living room window and saw the old doe walking by at a faster clip, stopping to graze on foliage, and most interesting to me was her demeanor. Her head was up. When I walked out to the backyard, she appeared alert and looked right at me before she went back to browsing. I walked back into the house, found Don and said, "I thought you were going to shoot the old doe?" Don nonchalantly replied, "I caught her and set her broken leg." "She isn't in pain now, and she is doing better." Yes, indeed. This morning on my birthday, I saw a beautiful thing!

Don is a very good man!

9 798330 268955